Case Examples in Child Welfare and Family Services for Social Workers

This book provides social work students at both undergraduate and graduate level with compelling child welfare case examples, intervention plans, and tips for building working alliances with clients.

The 50 such case examples, categorized by maltreatment type(s) and by underlying problem(s), each present an intertwined network of issues characterizing the members of a family and their interactions—as in actual field situations. Thus, social work students learning therapy or case management will find a wide variety of scenarios from child welfare services and children/family outpatient care and will learn about the range of challenges clients can face.

Using the instruction/practice sheets that illustrate sound approaches for joining with clients to tailor their own interventions, students are provided with the tools to work out the application of assessment and intervention strategies with regard to the particular circumstances of each example. Throughout, the emphasis is on growing the working alliance between social worker and client, reflecting the strength perspective emphasized in social work practice.

Tyrone Cheng spent two decades as a college professor, directing undergraduate and graduate programs and chairing social work departments for four universities, and for eight years worked in the American Midwest as a licensed social worker providing family preservation services and outpatient treatment. Cheng has authored 111 published and forthcoming refereed journal articles reporting his research in child welfare, intimate partner violence, mental health, and substance abuse.

Skills for Social Work Practice

This textbook series is ideal for all students studying to be qualified social workers, whether at undergraduate or postgraduate level. Covering key elements of the social work curriculum, the books are accessible, interactive, and thought-provoking.

New Titles

Case Examples in Child Welfare and Family Services for Social Workers
Tyrone Cheng

https://www.routledge.com/Skills-for-Social-Work-Practice/book-series/SSW

Case Examples in Child Welfare and Family Services for Social Workers

Tyrone Cheng

Routledge
Taylor & Francis Group

LONDON AND NEW YORK

Designed cover image: © Getty Images

First published 2023
by Routledge
4 Park Square, Milton Park, Abingdon, Oxon OX14 4RN

and by Routledge
605 Third Avenue, New York, NY 10158

Routledge is an imprint of the Taylor & Francis Group, an informa business

© 2023 Tyrone Cheng

The right of Tyrone Cheng to be identified as author of this work has been asserted in accordance with sections 77 and 78 of the Copyright, Designs and Patents Act 1988.

British Library Cataloguing-in-Publication Data
A catalogue record for this book is available from the British Library

Library of Congress Cataloging-in-Publication Data
Names: Cheng, Tyrone, author.
Title: Case examples in child welfare and family services for social workers / Tyrone Cheng.
Description: Abingdon, Oxon ; New York, NY : Routledge, 2023. | Includes bibliographical references and index. |
Identifiers: LCCN 2022022947 (print) | LCCN 2022022948 (ebook) | ISBN 9781032327822 (hbk) | ISBN 9781032327549 (pbk) | ISBN 9781003316688 (ebk)
Subjects: LCSH: Child welfare. | Social service.
Classification: LCC HV713 .C378 2023 (print) | LCC HV713 (ebook) | DDC 362.7--dc23/eng/20220603
LC record available at https://lccn.loc.gov/2022022947
LC ebook record available at https://lccn.loc.gov/2022022948

ISBN: 978-1-032-32782-2 (hbk)
ISBN: 978-1-032-32754-9 (pbk)
ISBN: 978-1-003-31668-8 (ebk)

DOI: 10.4324/9781003316688

Typeset in Sabon
by MPS Limited, Dehradun

Contents

Figures

Acknowledgments

I express sincere thanks to the people who have made this book possible. First off, my warmest thanks go to my wife, Celia, for love and support she has always given me. I am also especially grateful to the many clients and students who have taught me so much over the years. I owe a great debt of gratitude as well to my former colleagues at the University of Alabama at Birmingham and the University of Alabama, in Tuscaloosa. And may I thank Debra Peters, for constructive advice about my practice in an intensive family preservation program in Michigan; Chris Walker, for showing confidence in my ability to successfully apply experiences in child welfare services to the teaching of BSW students; and the campus library at the University of Alabama in Tuscaloosa, which provides excellent and comprehensive services.

1 Introduction

This book provides social work students at an undergraduate or graduate level with compelling case examples and intervention plans, plus advice for building sound working alliances with clients. It is for social workers in child welfare services, children and family services, and community-based social services (and also for future therapists and case managers). It will help students prepare to encounter a multiplicity of challenging situations in child welfare services and in children and family outpatient services.

Case examples appear in Chapters 2, 3, and 4, grouped by maltreatment type and by underlying problem. Each case example presents a network of intertwining issues characterizing a family's members and their interactions—as in actual field situations. These issues include physical, sexual, emotional, or other maltreatment; various mental disorders; and apparently incompatible developmental tasks. Social work students interested in providing therapy or case management will find here many examples from child welfare and children and family outpatient care, speaking to the range of difficulties real clients face. Each example is an opportunity to create—using the worksheet and guidance provided—an effective assessment strategy, and to develop the best intervention plan in light of the case's particulars. To study this book is to gain tools for steering clients to a desirable outcome.

I built the book's case examples on my practice with over 300 families since obtaining the MSW and PhD in social work. As a licensed social worker, I am keenly aware of my responsibility to advance clients' safety and desirable outcomes. Competent social workers, I believe, possess the skills to build working alliances with clients, since clients' commitment to safety and change stems from alliance with the social worker. Exposure to case examples in this book will hone those skills. Chapter 5 explicitly presents the essentials of building working alliances; without working alliance, no amount of therapeutic expertise can secure desirable outcomes.

While my case examples are indeed glimpses of real-life practice, I have chosen not to include clients' racial/ethnic backgrounds. Readers or course instructors can assign such backgrounds to individuals in the examples as needed. This will create opportunity for students to become mindful of pervasive racial/ethnic stereotyping and cultural norms. Case examples might also be modified to reflect students' communities, for instance, urban or rural, within the United States or outside it. Modification can engage students in exploring their local resources and practicing both critical thinking and engagement skills. Readers will see that certain case examples include a *later development*. Each *later development* discusses something happening to or with a client after an intervention starts; each tests students' reactions or responses (that is,

DOI: 10.4324/9781003316688-1

can they rework intervention plans efficiently to suit unfolding events?). The addenda simulate the unexpected—to which we are continually subject as we guide our clients.

Chapter 6 features intervention plans presenting productive approaches for joining with clients to tailor their own interventions. Chapter 7 presents concepts manifested in the self-monitoring log, along with procedures for its use. Chapter 7 also covers the *daily diary*, meant for clients' use as they assume accountability for their own behavioral changes. Chapters 6 and 7 emphasize building of working alliance between social worker and client, stressing the strength perspective from the literature on social work practice.

I designed this book for faculty, field instructors, students, and practitioners. I have used its case examples often in teaching social work to undergraduates and graduate students at several universities across two decades. I scrutinized these examples (as can any social work teacher) with my students completing courses in child welfare services, family preservation services, evidence-based practice, practice-focused research methods, and human behavior in the social environment. Students welcomed the case examples and even shared them in other courses, during class discussions. The examples prove so intriguing because they let students peek into the realities of the practice they will soon step into.

Using this book, no narrow focus on a particular therapeutic model constricts students' insights. Instead, the merits of *any* therapeutic model(s) promising utility in light of the case example's details can be deliberated. The case examples and guidance this book offers are supported by what I learned as a researcher as well as a licensed social worker. My 111 published and forthcoming titles include 27 focused on child welfare services. The research studies reported in my publications reflect data drawn from national datasets or obtained from nonprofit community-based social-service agencies.

2 Case Examples in Child Welfare Services

2.1 Neglect—Anthony; Cider; Dolittle; JJ; Ken and Hana; Renee

2.1.1 Anthony

Anthony was a one-month-old infant of Mark (age 19) and Joan (age 18). Mark and Joan lived together for a year. When Anthony attended a regular checkup, the attending pediatrician filed a report of failure-to-thrive to Child Protective Services (CPS). The pediatrician found no medical or biological causes why Anthony gained little weight. The CPS investigated and substantiated the report. The court ordered that Anthony remain at home with his parents but that the parents must attend intensive family services. CPS supervised the family.

The family was living in a one-bedroom apartment. The apartment was cluttered and the floor was dirty. However, there was no apparent health hazard or offensive odor. The utilities were functioning properly. The young couple was evicted from their former apartment for unpaid back rent. They secured this apartment with the Section 8 voucher. The family had no phone or family car. There was only one bottle for Anthony and it apparently was not clean. Joan did not breast-feed Anthony, but there was only one small can of formula left.

When the social worker visited the family, Mark was playing video games. He appeared to be apathetic to the intervention from the court and CPS. However, when Joan asked him to get the bottle, he became so angry that he threw the bottle at the floor; the bottle landed only two feet from where Anthony was sleeping. Mark did not show any affection to or even look at Anthony. Mark did not know how to hold Anthony in his arms.

Since Mark dropped out from high school, he had no stable employment. Mark revealed that he and his brothers were charged for car theft. His parents bailed him and his brothers out but they offered no further help. He would attend a court hearing in next month. He worried that he could be incarcerated for several years if he was found guilty. He reportedly used marijuana with his friends weekly, but he did not smoke marijuana in this apartment or in front of Anthony.

Although Joan did graduate from high school, she could find only part-time jobs. She quit her job upon becoming pregnant. Joan appeared to be healthy but tired. She felt overwhelmed by the financial problem and family situation. She did not know how to take care of Anthony and she was worried about his health. She worried about Mark's temper. Reportedly, Mark sometimes threw objects (including pictures) in the apartment after he drank a few beers. On several occasions, he yelled at her and

DOI: 10.4324/9781003316688-2

cornered her because she asked him to help her in some housekeeping chores. She believed that she could not take good care of Anthony all by herself. Mark spending years in jail and her having to raise Anthony alone were fearful prospects for her. Joan did not use any substance or drugs.

Joan's parents (Dennis and Carmen) wanted to help Joan and Anthony. Dennis, a military officer, believed that Mark was a bad person and that Mark ruined Joan's plan of joining the Air Force. Joan reportedly might still carry out that plan in a few years. Joan did not invite her parents to the apartment because she was afraid that Dennis would find out Mark's temper and consequently harm Mark. Joan had not contacted her good friends since she started living with Mark.

Anthony reportedly cried a lot, day and night. Joan could not understand the reason for his crying. Holding Anthony did not necessarily stop his crying. Joan showed affection to Anthony, but she was also nervous. Anthony once had a fever so high that Joan begged her next-door neighbor to drive her to get some over-the-counter medicine. Mark reportedly was taking a nap when that incident happened.

2.1.2 Cider Family

Harold (age 48) and Lela (age 42) were parents of seven children. The infant's toes were bitten by roaches and became infected. One night the infant was crying so badly that Lela took the infant to the emergency room. The physician removed a roach from the infant's ear and filed a report with child protective services. The investigation substantiated the charges of neglect. The apartment reportedly was infested by roaches. Harold and Lela were willing to correct their problems so that the infant and children would not be removed from the home. They agreed to cooperate with family preservation services.

The family was living in a basement apartment with three bedrooms. The apartment had couple of small, narrow windows near the top of the wall. The outside of the window was covered with a thin layer of dust that sunlight was barely able to come through. The air was stuffy in the apartment. The concrete floor was covered by a thin layer of dust or dirt. Roaches, in a variety of sizes, were crawling around everywhere in the apartment. However, there was no food crumb or leftovers around, and the kitchen was clean. The parents and infant occupied one bedroom. Four boys occupied a large room. In the middle of this "bedroom" was a gas water heater. Two girls occupied another small bedroom. Bunk beds had sufficient mattresses and blankets. In the living room were two old, torn sofas. The only bathroom was not clean and the toilet apparently could not flush. The water, however, came out the tap weakly. Shower tub was scattered with mold.

Harold and Lela were married 19 years and they had no prior relationships or marriages. They reported no history of mental health problems, substance use, or criminal activities. Harold had been a maintenance worker for many years. His meager monthly income was barely sufficient for the family expenses. Lela did not work and took care of the children at home. Several years ago, the family was evicted from a former residence because they were behind on rent. Since they could afford only this apartment, they did not complain the conditions of this apartment.

The children reportedly had good academic performance at school. They studied and did their homework in a community center because of the limited space at home.

They did not invite their friends to their home. At home, the siblings had occasional arguments and conflict. Lela usually could settle their problems.

2.1.3 Dolittle Family

2.1.3.1 Reasons for Referral

Gwen (age 30) and Brandon (age 33) were married for eight years. They had two children—Robert (age 8) and April (age 4). They were living in a three-bedroom house. CPS found animal feces in the children's bedrooms, the bathroom, and the basement. The family had two dogs and two cats. Trash and a strong offensive odor were found throughout the house. The refrigerator was empty and there were only a few boxes of cereal in the kitchen cupboard. The electricity at their home had been off for three months because of an outstanding bill of $500. CPS substantiated the neglect charges against Gwen and Brandon.

CPS allowed Robert and April to remain with their parents only if the parents could rectify the house conditions as soon as possible. The family was referred to the family agency by CPS.

2.1.3.2 Social History

Gwen was the biological mother of the two children. She was raised by her mother and stepfather. She had one stepbrother and one sister. Her stepfather allegedly sexually abused Gwen and her older sister. When she was 15 years old, she ran away from home and never returned. She became a prostitute and was arrested at age 20. She had quit her drug addiction. Two years later, she attended night school and eventually obtained her GED. She worked second shift five days per week in a packing company.

One year later, she met and married Brandon. When she was pregnant with April, Brandon accused her of adultery and beat her. She did not call the police. Six months ago, Brandon dropped out from their marital counseling. Gwen considered pursuing a divorce.

Gwen had hallucinations and was scared. Gwen reportedly saw her stepfather and heard his voices more than one year ago. She sought help from a psychiatrist six months ago. She had quit taking the prescription because she could not afford it, despite the prescription had stopped her hallucinations.

Gwen also had depression. She slept less than four hours a day. She lost her appetite. She cried easily and felt tired. She held negative perceptions of events that happened to her. The recent crises were overwhelming and stressful for her.

Gwen had the major share of childcare responsibility. She walked Robert to school every day. She alone took her children to medical and dental appointments.

In the last six months, she was the sole income earner for the family. The family had many unpaid bills. They were three months behind in house payments. She did not apply for Temporary Assistance for Needy Families (TANF) and refused to depend on welfare. She believed that their financial burden would be relieved if Brandon got a job.

Brandon was raised by his parents who were alcoholic. He recalled hardship and physical abuse in his childhood. He perceived himself as the "black sheep" of the family. He expected no help from his parents or brothers. He dropped out of high school to take a job. He later obtained his GED. He had been working in many different jobs until six months ago, when he complained that he had sharp pain at his stomach.

Brandon had been an alcoholic. He had been drinking two six-packs of beer per day for years after Gwen had an affair. Brandon reported that Gwen had left him for Jeff and had come back to him only after she found that Jeff was worse than him. Brandon was arrested for Driving Under the Influence (DUI) several times. He had attended several AA meetings two years ago but did not find them helpful to him. The social worker smelled alcohol on Brandon's breath.

Robert appeared to be developmentally on target for his age. He attended the second grade and did not like his classmates because they made fun of him. He frequently got out of his seat and talked to his friend in class. His teachers sent him to the hallway or principal's office numerous times. He and his friend fought and harassed other students together. The school counselor suggested testing for Robert's attention deficit hyperactivity disorder (ADHD) symptoms, but parents rejected the suggestion because of the rumors regarding the medication for ADHD.

April attended Head Start. Her speech was unclear, and she also had a hearing problem. She easily cried and had a temper tantrum. She kicked and bit others. She and Robert physically fought over toys and other matters. She wet her bed every night. Gwen had applied prescription shampoo to control head lice in April's hair.

The parents were impatient with their children. They believed that physical punishment was the best method to manage the misbehavior of Robert and April.

Brandon stated that he was the only person in the house to clean the house. However, the house was in a filthy condition when the social worker first visited the home. The carpet was covered with numerous stains and had a strong offensive odor. The floor and carpet in every room were scattered with animal feces. The odor and stains appeared to be due to animal feces and urine. The kitchen sink was piled up with dirty dishes and a layer of dirty water. The kitchen was infested with roaches.

2.1.4 JJ

Britney (age 22), a single mother gave birth to a baby boy, JJ. The pediatrician diagnosed JJ of failure-to-thrive and reported to CPS. JJ was hospitalized and CPS investigated. CPS records showed that two years ago Britney's first baby was died of sudden infant death syndrome (SIDS). CPS decided to remove JJ from Britney's care and placed him in a foster home after discharged from the hospital. JJ has regained some weight and he was returned to Britney, with a social worker from family preservation program assigned to the family.

Britney revealed that two years ago she was drinking in the evening; when she returned home, she went to sleep with her baby boy. She found him dead the next morning. The coroner determined that the cause of baby's death was SIDS. She was very vague whether she was intoxicated that evening.

JJ had gastrointestinal problem that he could not ingest milk. A special medical device was attached outside his stomach so that he could be fed through a tube to the device at his stomach. The pediatrician prescribed that JJ needed to be fed every four hours with a specific number of ounces of a specific formula. He needed to gain one ounce each day to regain normal weight. The social worker helped Britney obtain the special formula, baby supplies, and Special Supplemental Nutrition Program for Women, Infants, and Children (WIC) coupons.

The social worker recommended community nurse services and the pediatrician prescribed the service. A community visiting nurse demonstrated to Britney how to appropriately feed JJ. The social worker helped Britney to use self-monitoring log in documentation of feeding JJ. The community visiting nurse weighed JJ twice per week with the same scale. The social worker visited the family daily and provided emotional support and other interventions. In the first week of intervention, Britney recorded her feeding regularly and JJ's weight records showed some gains. However, on the first day of the second week of intervention, Britney missed two feedings. Britney began to complain the difficulty of waking up and feeding JJ at 2 a.m. A respite babysitter was arranged for eight hours on the next day. On the weekend, Britney insisted that she needed the respite babysitter again because she needed a break—having a drink with her friends in a bar. She denied that she had any drinking problem. Nevertheless, the records of feeding and weighing appeared to agree with each other.

Britney often did not hold JJ. She put him in a car seat on the floor and she rocked the car seat with her foot. She claimed that JJ cried if she held him. When the social worker held and rocked JJ in his arms, JJ was calm and fell asleep quickly. Britney refused to play with JJ because it was not her way of showing affection. After another week of intervention, Britney used the respite babysitter again. Britney reported regular feedings and JJ's weight records appeared to grow as prescribed. However, Britney continued to have no physical attachment or emotional bonding with JJ.

In the fourth week, a friend of Britney reported that Britney did not feed JJ regularly but fed him extra amount on the days of community-nurse visit. Britney admitted that she only committed such behaviors once because she was using marijuana. When this social worker reported Britney's marijuana use, the CPS caseworker told Britney not to use marijuana again and JJ was remained in Britney's care.

2.1.4.1 Later Development

After five weeks of intervention (agency's limit), the pediatrician was satisfied with the growing rate of JJ. However, the social worker believed that Britney would not continue to feed JJ regularly without parental bonding or attachment with JJ. The social worker recommended removal of JJ from Britney. Based on the pediatrician's recommendations that JJ had gained normal growth, the court decided that JJ returned to Britney without court supervision. Britney agreed that she would comply with a follow-up service—a less intensive in-home services—recommended by the social worker.

2.1.5 *Ken and Hanna*

It was reported to CPS that the family's home was filthy. CPS investigated and substantiated the report. The parents, Ken (age 27) and Hanna (age 22), have agreed to keep their home clean from now on and also to accept family preservation services.

Ken and Hanna have two children, Austin (age 5) and Lily (6 months old). The family lives with its pet dog in a two-bedroom house. The house has a strong and offensive odor. Dropped food and other garbage, including animal feces, is scattered on the carpeted floor. Half-empty soda cans and baby bottles sit atop the furniture, and dirty dishes are piled in the kitchen sink—which does not drain and thus is filled with dirty water. The kitchen table is covered with empty food packages and leftover food. The full trashcan has no lid.

In the bathroom, human feces can be seen on the floor. The toilet and bathtub, though functional, are filthy. The parents' bedroom, where Lily's crib is located, is relatively clean; the dog is not allowed in this room. Austin's bedroom is littered with toys, clothes, and other objects.

Hanna reported no abuse or neglect in her childhood. At age 17 she became pregnant with Austin and she dropped out from high school. When she was working, Hanna's mother was Austin's caregiver. John (aged 17) is the biological father of Austin, but he moved away and never supported Austin. Ken is the biological father of Lily. Before Lily was conceived, Hanna had a miscarriage. Ken and Hanna do not wish to have any more children.

As a high school student, Hanna was diagnosed with mild mental retardation. She can read and write, and she is responsive in a conversation. Her appearance is dirty—her feet are very dirty and she has a strong body odor. She is a part-time worker at a neighborhood fast-food restaurant.

At age two Ken suffered brain damage when his skull was fractured in a car accident. After his parents divorced, he and his siblings were raised by their grandmother Loraine (age 74) and their biological father, Malcolm, Loraine's son. Ken reported no child abuse or neglect in his childhood. He said his grandmother and father closely restricted the places he could go as a child. Malcolm passed away one year ago.

Ken completed high school, after which he worked in fast-food restaurants for two years. He stopped working when he became ill with gall bladder disease. He remains unemployed, although he occasionally does odd jobs. He and Hanna share household expenses. Ken instructs Hanna to supervise their children and complete the household chores, but he rarely contributes to household chores. Hanna expects Ken to make the major decisions for the family. Currently, the family is using a van loaned to them by Loraine. Ken is the only person in the household who can drive.

Ken supervises both children when Hanna is at work. He has difficulty changing Lily's diaper unassisted. Lily wears a wet or soiled diaper for extended periods before being cleaned and changed by Hanna. Ken does not take the children or Hanna along when he visits his relatives.

Lily appears to be healthy and playful. Austin is active and playful too, but his appearance is filthy and his speech is unclear. In addition, he cries easily and is prone to throwing temper tantrums on the floor. He attends a preschool program for developmental delays.

Ken and Hanna have complained that Austin always challenges their authority, refusing to follow instructions and having many temper tantrums. Both parents show limited knowledge of parenting skills; they unsuccessfully used time-out technique to manage Austin's undesirable behavior. They give instructions to Austin while they are sitting in chairs. Austin does not comply with acceptable bedtimes, staying up typically until near midnight; he does not like afternoon nap time. Hanna sometimes works on household chores after midnight. Ken stays up all night, often arises after 1 p.m. On weekends, when Austin wakes by himself before either parent wakes, he leaves his bedroom and wanders in the house; in response, the parents often lock him in his bedroom. Furthermore, Austin does not use the toilet properly and does not clean himself after defecating on the bathroom floor. Ken reports he feels sick when he must clean up after Austin in the bathroom. Hanna is not affected physically by that task, but she feels overwhelmed by her work schedule and the chores.

Loraine, who is in good health, is reportedly supportive of Ken's young family. She has been delegated to handle his Supplemental Security Income (SSI) checks and other financial documents. She helped the family obtain the low-rent home they live in. Loraine lives in the next town and occasionally visits the family (in addition, the family does laundry at Loraine's home). She said that Hanna is not a competent parent or housekeeper.

The family receives food stamps and cash benefits from TANF.

2.1.6 Renee

Renee (age 42) was a single mother of Katie (age 16) and Paul (age 10). Renee was the youngest in her family and she was never abused or neglected in her childhood. She had three brothers living in another state. Renee and David (age 45) married for six years and they divorced. After the divorce four years earlier, Renee and her children moved in with her maternal grandparents. The grandparents eventually passed away and left the house to Renee. David had not been paying child support.

Renee graduated from high school and was trained as a nurse's aide. One year ago, she injured her back badly at work. After she had five back operations, she was able to walk around without any assistance. She took many medications and saw several specialists for the pain on her back. Since she lost the job in the nursing home, she had worked four minimum-wage jobs. She worked long hours seven days per week.

At home, the washer had recently broken down but Renee could not afford the repairs. The family had 15 dogs, nine cats, and five birds. Animal feces were everywhere. Strong and offending odors were observable in the house. Dirty dishes were piled up in the sink and trash was on the floor. Toilets were not working properly. School teachers filed reports to CPS because of the children's consistent odor on their clothing. After CPS investigated and substantiated the filthy and unhealthy conditions at home, the court had ordered Renee to clean up the house within two weeks. While Renee was putting a large volume of trash outside her house, her neighbors complained about the odor and the city had given her a ticket for dumping trash. She felt very frustrated that no one was trying to help her. She felt hopeless and was fearful that children would be removed from her.

Katie appeared to be age-appropriate in her development. She cried when she talked about her family situation. She felt very shameful for the insanitary condition of her home. She did not want any people to visit her home. Although she got A's and B's in school, she did not have any friends. She complained that Renee did not spend time with her, and said that Renee spent long hours at work or slept a lot at home.

Paul was diagnosed with ADHD but he had quit taking the psychotherapeutic medication for months because Renee could not afford it. He did not follow Renee's instructions. He was impulsive and hyperactive at home. He felt bored at home but he enjoyed playing with the animals there.

2.2 Physical Abuse—Carter; Walter

2.2.1 Carter Family

Trenton (age 10) was reported to the CPS when his teacher found bruises on his arms and marks on his face. CPS investigated and substantiated that father Mr. Carter physically abused Trenton. Trenton was removed from his father's home and placed in a foster home for six months. Mr. Carter completed all the recommended services and Trenton returned home last week. The family was still under supervision of the court. CPS referred the family to IJK family preservation services.

Mr. Carter was a single parent. He and his wife divorced three years ago because she abused cocaine. Mr. Carter gained custody of Trenton, and his ex-wife moved to another state. Mr. Carter was a Coast Guard officer before the divorce. He had a college degree but became a security guard of a local mall. He reportedly enjoyed his work.

Mr. Carter was very frustrated by Trenton's behavior before his removal. Reportedly, Trenton often lied about his schoolwork and had poor grades at school. He often played video games after school at home before his father came home from work. Mr. Carter believed that Trenton was very capable of getting good grades but was lazy. Mr. Carter became so frustrated that he spanked Trenton with a wooden spoon, slapped Trenton's face, and hit Trenton with his fist. Mr. Carter regretted this physical punishment and was very happy that he had regained custody of Trenton. From parenting classes, Mr. Carter learned some behavior management skills for parenting Trenton and he understood Trenton's psychology better. Mr. Carter's hobby was playing video games at night. He had no new romantic relationship since the divorce.

Trenton was happy that he was reunited with his father. He had a positive experience in the foster home. He regretted that he lied to his father in the past. He revealed that he did not like schoolwork and sometimes found it very difficult. He did not like school because other students often teased him about being chubby. He enjoyed playing video games and could spend hours in talking about them. He reported that he and his father rarely spent quality time together.

Trenton reported that he did not miss his mother and had fearful experiences with his mother's erratic behavior. His mother occasionally called him but he did not like to talk to her. Mr. Carter was worried that his ex-wife would contest his custody of Trenton. Mr. Carter strongly believed that his ex-wife was still a drug addict, and Mr. Carter revealed that he did not like his ex-wife calling Trenton.

2.2.2 Walter

Bobby (age 25) and Mary (age 23) have been married for two years. Walter (age 4 months) is their first child. At two months old, Walter was hospitalized and diagnosed with a subdural hematoma. CPS investigated Walter's injury. Bobby admitted to the investigators that he had accidentally dropped Walter on the floor. Walter was then placed in the care of his maternal grandmother, Emma. Supervised by Emma, Bobby and Mary have been having visitations with Walter. Walter's reunification with his parents is being considered. Bobby and Mary were referred to ABC family preservation services for an assessment of safe reunification.

Reportedly, Bobby and Mary have a strongly bonded spousal relationship. Mary finds Bobby to be a caring husband and father and believes him when he says Walter fell accidentally. Mary and Bobby maintain a close relationship with Emma. Bobby's brother and sister-in-law occasionally come to Emma's home to play with Walter.

As a child, Bobby was physically abused by his biological parents. He was removed from their home and placed in a series of foster homes until he aged out of services. Bobby's first marriage reportedly ended due to his ex-wife's infidelity. No violence was evident in this initial spousal relationship. Bobby works today as a bricklayer for a construction company. A typical day of work leaves him tired. He consumes a 12-ounce beer once or twice a month. Reportedly he had consumed no alcohol on the day Walter fell. Bobby is softspoken and always appears very calm.

Mary was never abused or neglected by her parents. Mary completed high school. She had worked prior to Walter's birth. Afterwards, she cared for Walter in her home full-time. Mary's father passed away some 18 months before Walter's birth. She has experienced sadness over his passing, having occasional crying spells and sleep difficulties. Mary has not sought professional help for this sadness. She does not consume any alcohol or recreational drugs. She has no reported history of hallucinations or suicidal ideation.

The family's two-bedroom apartment is clean and tidy; all its utilities function properly. Baby mobiles are hanging near Walter's crib; toy rattles appear on an area rug that covers part of the floor. For part of his five months, Walter suffered from severe colic, crying for an hour every night. Bobby and Mary took turns attending to him when he was colicky. Walter now takes prescribed medication treating his colic.

Walter's physician confirms that the baby recovered quickly from the subdural hematoma. Walter is alert, responsive, and playful; no difficulties with his eye movement or hearing are apparent. Walter can roll over independently. He can raise his upper body by pushing against the floor with his arms.

During visitation with Walter, Bobby and Mary both reportedly demonstrate care for and affection toward Walter. Bobby often holds Walter in his arms and gently rocks Walter. Both parents, however, lack sufficient knowledge about typical development in one- to three-year-old children (e.g., cognition, language, and fine-motor skills).

2.2.2.1 Later Development

When Mary went for a visitation with Walter unaccompanied by Bobby, she was beside the crying Walter. Suddenly, she picked Walter up by one leg, letting him hang upside down, at which he cried even more loudly. A family preservation therapist participating in the visitation immediately stopped Mary's behavior and then reported it to CPS. During the investigation, Bobby revealed that he had not dropped Walter either accidentally or on purpose. Instead, he had arrived home from work one evening to find Mary crying and allegedly shaking Walter upside down. Bobby secured the baby, and he and Mary took Walter to the emergency room at once.

2.3 Sexual Abuse—Jill; Michelle

2.3.1 Jill

Jill (age 31) is a single mother and has neither a high school diploma nor any work experience. At age 19, she moved out of her parents' home. She has relied on public assistance since then, for herself and three children. The children have different fathers, but none of their fathers pays child support or is otherwise involved with his child. The family—which includes Jill's boyfriend, Mel—lives in a public housing project and does not have a car for transportation.

Maple (age 7) has started showing signs of language and cognitive delays. Her teachers believe Maple to be "retarded." Her classmates often laugh at her, and she has become easily angered, wanting to fight others at school.

Luke (age 11) has become physically aggressive, frequently fighting with other children from the housing project during their outdoor play. Jill often gets into arguments with other parents in the housing project. She claims her neighbors are drug addicts, and she dislikes them. She also complains the housing project is full of "gang-bangers" who sell drugs.

Linda (age 10) once told Jill that Mel had touched her private area. Jill did not believe what Linda said. Jill believes Mel when he asserts his innocence concerning Linda, and Jill does not want him to leave.

2.3.2 Michelle

Michelle (36) and her three children—Karen (age 18), Nicole (age 12), and Oliver (age 11)—as well as Larry (age 2) (Karen's child) live together in an apartment. Nicole and Oliver are Karen's stepsiblings. Karen's father and Michelle had a brief relationship which ended before Karen was born. Michelle used to live with Nicole and Oliver's father, Patrick (age 35), along with Karen and the children.

One year ago, Karen told Michelle that Patrick had sexually touched her private areas. Michelle believed that Karen was lying and ignored her. Karen then reported Patrick's behavior to her teacher, who filed a report with CPS. During CPS's investigation, Patrick said that Karen had seduced him and he had touched her sexually. The court would not allow Patrick to continue living with the family unless he completed psychological evaluation and treatment. He now lives several blocks away from the family.

Patrick believes that he did nothing wrong, accusing Karen of seducing him. He has no interest in being evaluated and treated by a psychologist. He has demanded supervised visitations on Saturdays only, saying he is too tired for visits after work during the week. Patrick works as a courier driver and continues to pay the family's expenses; Michelle has also been working part-time for about six months. Patrick has been vague about his history of substance use.

Michelle and Patrick believe that the court has no right to separate them. Michelle blames the entire incident and its fallout on Karen's "promiscuity." Michelle herself sees Patrick frequently. Although she suspects him of having become involved with another woman, she wants to reunite with him.

Karen feels overwhelmed by her family's situation. She and Quinn, Larry's father, broke up about two months ago. Karen had been frustrated by Quinn's lack of interest in helping care for Larry. Karen herself appears to have little knowledge of infant care. She has had difficulty calming Larry. Michelle has provided little help with the baby, telling Karen he is her responsibility. Karen attended school sporadically last year but dropped out during the current year. She has a marginal IQ score but was never diagnosed with mental retardation.

Karen remains afraid of Patrick and has had nightmares about the molestation.

Three weeks ago, she was very frightened when Patrick knocked on the door. She locked him out and hid in her room for several hours.

Nicole and Oliver appear to be healthy and developing appropriately for their age. They earn good grades and have many friends at school. They miss Patrick and they blame Karen for the separation.

2.4 Abandonment—Lucy

2.4.1 Lucy

Lucy (age 22) became a runaway at age 13, which brought her into the juvenile justice system, but its intervention did not stop Lucy from running away again.

Lucy is a single parent of Maya (age 7), Mario (age 4), and Simon (age 3). Maya was born when Lucy was only 15 years old and involved in a relationship with a 26-year-old man. After becoming pregnant, she quit the GED classes she was taking.

Lucy's parents, Catholics, were angered by this pregnancy. The alcoholic father had physically abused Lucy when she was younger, and the mother's relationship with Lucy had always been a distant one. Eventually, Lucy's parents moved out of state. They left Lucy and baby Maya in the care of Joan, Lucy's aunt. At age 18, Lucy left her aunt's home. She then had two brief relationships with men and gave birth to Mario and Simon.

Since leaving her aunt's place, Lucy has had no stable home for family. They have stayed for brief periods with Lucy's friends or boyfriends. She had no income of her own until she began getting TANF aid some years ago. Through TANF, she secured an apartment, and she also participated in job training, although the training has not led to her employment. Lucy's TANF benefits have now run out, and she has lost her apartment. The family is back to sheltering for short periods with different friends.

About two months ago, one of those friends contacted CPS when Lucy went off, leaving the children at the friend's home and failing to reappear for several days. CPS removed and placed the children in three different foster homes. Lucy's other legal troubles include a shoplifting conviction and fines for being an unlicensed and uninsured driver. She owes over $500 in fines.

At age 13 Lucy had begun using marijuana. She is vague about when exactly she stopped using marijuana, but she denies having used any other illegal drugs. She has reported that at times she feels depressed; however, she has not sought treatment for her depressive moods.

During supervised visitations, Lucy and her children have exhibited affection for each other. Lucy wants her family reunited. Her homelessness and lack of income are obstacles to reunification. Lucy has contacts with Joan and her eldest brother.

2.5 Family Violence—Teka

2.5.1 Teka

Teka (age 16) and her mother were fighting about using the Internet at home. Teka allegedly threw a computer mouse at her mother and bruised her forehead. Mother allegedly pushed Teka down to the floor. Teka called CPS and filed an abuse report against her mother. When CPS investigated, the mother asserted that Teka was aggressive and should be placed in residential facilities or foster care. Teka then agreed to cooperate with her mother. CPS was concerned about the violence at home and referred the family to EFG family preservation services.

Teka was 5' 10" tall. She was as big and strong as her mother. She had rapid and severe mood swings. She could be very happy in the morning and became depressed and angry in the afternoon for no apparent reason. She perceived her mother as a worthless, overbearing person. She complained that her mother often became involved in abusive or dysfunctional relationships with men. She complained that her mother did not earn enough to provide well for the family. She did not like her mother to tell her to do chores, homework, or other things. She admitted that she enjoyed spending hours surfing the Internet and visiting chat rooms. She became angry if her mother asked her to stop or disconnect the phone line. She admitted that she would become physically aggressive toward her mother if provoked. She did not like school and did not want to go to school. She often missed school because of allegedly feeling sick or waking up late. She did not have friends at school or in the neighborhood. Her mother refused to talk about Teka's biological father but Teka always wanted to know him. Teka smoked cigarettes taken from her mother. She denied using any other substances.

Teka's mother was a coffee shop manager. Teka became hostile when her mother tried to wake her up before going to work. Mother received notes from school regarding Teka's truancy but mother felt helpless about that. She found that Teka was chatting in adult chat rooms and becoming involved in sexualized conversation. When the mother confronted Teka, they yelled at and shoved each other. When the mother broke off from the argument, Teka would continue yelling and going after her. In one instance, Teka followed her mother to her bedroom and threw a chair toward a dresser. The mother was afraid of Teka's hostility. Mother wanted to fight back but she was afraid of going to jail for that. Mother believed that Teka did not use any substances. Mother was a recovering alcoholic and she had abstained from alcohol for two years. She became involved in several abusive relationships several years ago, with Teka witnessing the abuse. Mother then became very cautious with relationships and would not tolerate any abuse.

2.6 Poor Parental Supervision—Max and Denny; Mimi

2.6.1 Max and Denny

2.6.1.1 Presenting Problems

Three months ago, Max (age 8) and Denny (age 6) were removed from their mother, Irene (age 26), by CPS due to neglect. Currently, the children live in a foster home of the CB Family Agency. The family was referred to CB in-home counseling services because the children's father, Stanley (age 32), is a potential caretaker for the children.

2.6.1.2 Father's History

Following his parents' divorce, Stanley was raised by his mother from age seven. He reported experiencing no abuse and no neglect during his childhood. He dropped out of school during the 11th grade, because of the development of his first intimate relationship.

After divorced from his first wife, he met Irene. Stanley and Irene went on to live together, but many separations and reunions marked their relationship over time. Stanley attributed many of their break-ups to Irene's repeated infidelity. Stanley and Irene eventually married, but they divorced two years later. Stanley stated that he has no interest in restoring his relationship with Irene.

Stanley served 18 months in jail for writing bad checks but was released a year ago. In jail, he earned a GED. During his imprisonment, Stanley and Irene's daughter, Val (aged 2), drowned in a pond behind the family home as Irene spent time with her friends indoors. Her friends insisted that Irene was not drinking and was not intoxicated when the incident occurred. When police and CPS investigated, the drowning was ruled accidental. Stanley holds Irene responsible for Val's death, rejecting Irene's latest proposal they reunite. Stanley has attended counseling to manage his anger over Val's death.

Stanley's criminal record has made it difficult to find steady work and housing. He lives with his mother in a two-story house. The landlord, however, does not allow children to reside in his rental property. Stanley's mother signed the lease on the house; she and Stanley share in paying the rent and bills.

For about two weeks, Stanley has been working full-time at an auto repair shop. Stanley reportedly wants to demonstrate his commitment and ability to raise Max and Denny. He is also seeking a safe home for himself and the children.

Stanley began using alcohol and marijuana as a teenager, but he reportedly stopped using marijuana several years ago. He reportedly never used marijuana more than twice monthly (1/16 of an ounce on each occasion). Stanley also said that he has avoided drinking for the past six months, because he came to dislike the feelings of fatigue and anger that alcohol induced. He reportedly used to drink six 12-ounce beers two times a week, sometimes getting intoxicated.

While Stanley lived with Irene and their children, his sister had been available to babysit the children on occasions. He believes that he can care for the boys on his own, with perhaps some help from his mother.

Stanley has visited Max and Denny twice a week since they were placed in foster care. He has demonstrated appropriate supervision and parenting of the children. Stanley reported using reasoning and timeouts to manage their misbehavior; he said that he does not use physical punishment. During visitations, Stanley is firm with the boys and they respond well to his instruction. The bonding between the children and Stanley appears strong. They enjoy building models and going places together, and the boys spontaneously show affection to Stanley.

Stanley rides a motorcycle with confederate flag designs on it. However, he drives a car when he visits his children. The boys' foster parents supervise these visits, but they allow Stanley and the boys to go off together on their own. The foster parents are confident that Max and Denny are safe in Stanley's care.

Stanley wants to take care of his children. For a period of nine months earlier in their lives, they had lived with Stanley only, an arrangement that reportedly was a success—until Irene requested the boys be returned to her care.

2.6.1.3 Mother's History

At eight years old, Irene went to live with a friend of her parents, who raised her from then on. There was reportedly little discipline in the friend's home. Irene described herself as a "tomboy" in her youth; she reportedly had many accidents required stitches. She was not required to do any chores. She now believes that she should be the one to do all household chores; her children should not have chores to do. Furthermore, she wants her children to spend a lot of time playing outdoors.

When Irene was living with the children, clothes and trash were scattered around on the floor. The children put food wrappers beneath couch cushions; neighbor children also felt free to drop trash anywhere in the home. Flies and roaches were numerous in the home. Irene's children and their friends had demolished window screens at home. Upstairs in the bedrooms, missing screens posed a safety issue for the children. Once while fighting with his brother, Max removed a window screen and tried to throw it outside. A window at the rear of the house was broken, with glass scattered in the adjacent part of the backyard. The landlord had threatened to evict the family several times.

Irene showed little control of her children's behavior. She offered no structured activities or chores for the children; the children typically did not even pick up after themselves. They fought with each other; Irene appeared unable to contain their fights. Max once kicked Irene because he perceived her to favor Denny in an ongoing fight. Another time, after being hit by Denny, Max displaced his anger onto a neighborhood boy and hit him.

Irene consumes at least 40 ounces of beer daily at home. Her hands sometimes tremble. She has blackouts about twice a week. She is angry with CPS because caseworkers blame her for Val's death. Irene tends to hold Max accountable for Val's death, feeling that Max should have saved his sister. When police eventually returned to the home to remove the boys from Irene's care, she was intoxicated and did not know their whereabouts. After detoxification in a hospital, Irene refused further substance abuse treatment or participation in Alcoholics Anonymous (AA).

Irene is a part-time worker in a fast-food restaurant near her home; her coworkers reportedly dislike her. She is angry over the loss of welfare benefits because of the removal of her children. She is angry that CPS would consider allowing the boys to live with Stanley. She said that Stanley uses marijuana.

2.6.1.4 Children's History

When Max and Denny were living with Irene, the boys were found living in unsanitary conditions and surviving on insufficient food. They had at times been left home alone and had been exposed to Irene's intoxication.

Max takes a prescribed antidepressant; moreover, he attends counseling to address his depression, defiance, and aggression. Max has both anger and guilt about Val's death, and he has nightmares related to the drowning. He reportedly had tried to save Val by holding onto her hand as she was slipping under the water, yelling vainly for help.

In the foster home, Max has refused to help with chores such as taking out the trash and putting dishes in the sink. In contrast, he said that he always takes care of Denny, and that no one else should have that duty. At school, Max punched a student who teased Denny about living in a foster home.

In the foster home, Denny has appeared hyperactive, running around continually, seemingly unable to be still. His attention span is short; he may begin to play with someone or something, but then he will switch suddenly to another item or person. He has similar behaviors at school. The foster parents reported that Denny has a bedwetting problem. Denny is very talkative; he likes his foster parents. Although Denny was playing outside when Val had her accident, he recalls no details. He said he misses his mother and does not understand the separation.

Both boys enjoy Stanley's visits, and they want to live with Stanley. Max has joyfully recounted (from a time when they lived together) an experience of playing with Stanley in a park.

2.6.1.5 Later Development

Stanley's search for an affordable, appropriate residence has not been successful. Stanley completed a drug screen and its result was positive for marijuana, but he denied using marijuana. Stanley was then referred to drug treatment, but he did not show up for his initial appointments. Two weeks' non-attendance led to suspension of Stanley's treatment by the clinic. Stanley restated his commitment to the boys. Soon he gained readmission to drug treatment, but following two consecutive absences from Narcotics Anonymous meetings, he was again suspended by the clinic.

2.6.2 Mimi

One year ago, Mimi (age 16) and Sammy (age 14) were removed from the home of their mother, Kay (age 38), and placed in foster care. The action resulted from Kay's insufficient supervision at home, Sammy's delinquency, and Mimi's truancy. Mimi and Sammy, however, ran away from the foster home, stealing a van for transportation. Before long, Sammy was picked up by the police; Mimi soon turned herself in. The two subsequently were placed in a residential facility, Kingdom Place, where Sammy remains. A new foster home became available for Mimi six months ago, and now she has been referred by CPS to a family service agency, concerning reunification with Kay.

Kay was raised by her father following her mother's childbirth-related death. Kay reported a happy childhood in which she suffered no abuse or neglect. When she was 12 years old, her father died and she was raised by her paternal aunt Marge. Kay, a high school graduate, has worked in various jobs. Most recently she was a factory worker for eight months, a job she quit seven months ago following an argument with a supervisor.

Kay has a history of dysfunctional, unstable relationships, having two ex-husbands and several ex-boyfriends. None of the ex-husbands paid child support. One ex-husband was an alcoholic and abusive. Kay filed police reports when he choked Kay and dragged her by her hair, then he served jail time. An ex-boyfriend frequently intoxicated on alcohol; slammed Sammy into a wall when Sammy provoked him. Kay called police, but charges against her ex-boyfriend were later dropped.

Following the removal of Mimi and Sammy to foster care, Kay moved in with Butch (age 57). She reportedly is engaged to him, and she currently relies on his income.

Kay started drinking at age 14 and has a history of alcohol abuse. She was drinking heavily two years ago, in the attempt to deal with frustration and a sense of helplessness in the face of Sammy's growing delinquency and aggression. She regularly drank (beer and/or liquor) to the point of passing out. She drank in front of her children. Kay reported, however, that in May of this year she stopped drinking, because she had realized her behavior was causing problems in her family.

Kay sought professional help to address her substance abuse and underwent drug assessment at EFG Clinic. A therapist confirmed Kay's attendance at group therapy and individual counseling, over four months; the therapist also confirmed Kay attended AA meetings. Kay's drug screens have been negative. Kay said that she has found group therapy to be helpful, because it led her to realize she was drinking to escape parenting-related difficulties. Kay is very confident that she will complete drug treatment, and she said that she will seek a job once she does.

One ex-boyfriend's friend allegedly sexually abused Mimi and Sammy. Kay was unaware of this until the children described the abuse to the staff at Kingdom Place. Two years ago, Sammy reportedly became very aggressive toward Kay, punching and kicking her frequently. He stopped attending school and started sneaking out during the night to party with friends. Kay sought help from the police and from Sammy's school; consequently, Sammy was sent to the detention center several times. Learning that Sammy had been abused suggested to Kay that Sammy's behavior embodied his displacement onto her of his anger over the abuse.

Mimi also began to refuse to attend school, staying at home or with a relative while school was in session, generally sleeping all day. Kay tolerated her excuses. Like Sammy, Mimi began sneaking out to join friends in the middle of the night to use alcohol and marijuana. While living with her mother, she typically smoked six to nine cigarettes at home daily. She smokes at school when she can.

Kay tried to thwart Mimi and Sammy's late-night roaming by staying up all night. That left her tired in the daytime. She eventually began to ask Jim to discipline her children upon their return from partying.

Mimi has been manipulative at home. She has interfered in Kay's relationships with those boyfriends she did not like. Mimi now perceives that her mother has been trying everything to make her and Sammy happy. Furthermore, Mimi likes to play a mother's role where Sammy is concerned, trying to tell him what to do. Mimi does not appear expressive and open. She did not tell Kay about the sexual abuse by Sammy's father's friend, nor has she told her about other incidents in which Kay's boyfriends tried to touch Mimi inappropriately.

In her second foster home, the foster parent confirmed that Mimi negotiated assignment of household chores in the foster home, ultimately leaving both Mimi and the foster parent content with arrangements. Mimi sometimes shares her feelings and appears to understand she must follow rules if she is to remain in the home. She has withstood the temptation to smoke while interacting with teenagers in the neighborhood. Mimi understands that being asked to leave this current foster home (or running away from it) will markedly diminish her chances of returning to Kay's home. She hopes that Sammy can move into this foster home.

The relationship between Mimi and Kay (and also between Mimi and Sammy) is so strong that Mimi is insecure about it. She used to sleep with Kay; upon placement at Kingdom Place, Mimi had a fear of separation from Kay. Early on at Kingdom Place, Mimi feared all strangers; her fear eventually diminished as she adjusted to life there. But in the second foster home, Mimi has again felt fearful, mostly at night. She reportedly worries about how Sammy is doing at Kingdom Place without her.

Butch's parents separated when he was three years old, and he was raised by his mother. He reported a happy childhood, but he dropped out of high school. Butch maintains sporadic contact with his brother.

Over the years, Butch has worked in restaurants and factories. He has held his current factory job for almost three years. His weekly income is reportedly sufficient to support a family of four; he reported he currently holds no debt.

Butch has had three marriages. Butch has a daughter from this first marriage, for whom he reportedly paid child support through her 18th birthday. Butch raised his son from the second marriage and maintains a close relationship and frequent contact with his son. The third marriage lasted two years, with Butch divorcing his wife following her numerous extramarital affairs.

Butch and Kay are engaged. Butch reportedly does not smoke, drink alcohol, or use illicit drugs. When this social worker asked Butch if he had a record of child abuse/neglect, he answered no, after thinking briefly.

Butch has never lived with Mimi and Sammy. He knows of their behavior from observation and from listening to Kay describe it; he said that he feels prepared for the responsibility. He has accompanied Kay to counseling sessions with the children in Kingdom Place. Moreover, he appears willing to join in family counseling conducted during home visits. Butch states that in his opinion, the priorities for Mimi are obeying rules and successfully completing her education.

Kay and Butch are living in Butch's three-bedroom trailer, with two bedrooms unused except as storage areas. Butch and Kay plan to clean out and furnish the bedrooms for the children, in anticipation of their return. Butch has owned and lived in the trailer for three years.

2.6.2.1 Later Development

The social worker contacted the CPS and requested an investigation of Butch's potential child maltreatment records. Prosecutor office found that Butch was a sex offender on parole. Butch reportedly insisted his innocence and claimed that his public defender misguided him to admit sexual abuse of a teenage girl. Despite such revelation, Kay believed in Butch's claim and intended to continue their relationship.

2.7 Delinquency—Jeremiah; Jose; McCool

2.7.1 Jeremiah

In March, Jeremiah (age 15) accidentally fired a BB gun through the bathroom window at his home, and the pellet struck a 12-year-old neighbor boy in the face. The boy's parents pressed charges. Jeremiah completed six months of probation as well as a diversion program. More recently, while at school Jeremiah repeatedly punched a fellow student who had taunted Jeremiah because Jeremiah had carried out a teacher's direction to awaken a student sleeping at a desk, by poking the student with his finger. He was sent to the principal and subsequently arrested by a police officer. Guilty of a misdemeanor in this incident, Jeremiah was ordered by the court to complete one-year probation, an anger management course, and 20 hours of community service. The court also has ordered that the BCD Agency complete a family assessment for Jeremiah's family, prior to a disposition hearing.

Jeremiah's parents, Tammy (age 40) and Liam (age 42), separated and eventually divorced, four years ago. Since then Tammy has been taking care of Jeremiah and his sister, Alicia (age 12). The children have had no contact at all with Liam since the divorce. Because of jobs and relationship problems, Tammy moved her family eight times before settling at their current address. Two years ago, Tammy was engaged, and she and the children lived with her fiancé, Tom. However, Tom ultimately left Tammy for another woman. Jeremiah and Alicia were displeased with Tammy's decision to move into the present location.

Jeremiah displays impulsive and aggressive behavior. He shows no respect for rules and has little concern for the consequences of his actions. He appears to violate school rules intentionally and willfully, appearing to want to be caught and frequently laughing about it when he is. He shows little respect for teachers and other authority figures. For arguing with teachers about class assignments, he has received some 10 lunch-period detentions in one semester. Additionally, Jeremiah's impulsiveness was demonstrated by his purchase (from a fellow student and on school grounds) of an explosive device—an M-85; and by another incident in which he filled a two-liter bottle with gasoline and ignited it in his backyard. Jeremiah reportedly was fascinated by the exploding M-85 and gasoline-filled bottle in his backyard. One neighbor has complained repeatedly about Jeremiah's "disruptive" behavior. Jeremiah reportedly does not drink alcoholic beverages, smoke, use drugs, or have any interest in or ties to youth gangs.

Jeremiah makes D and F grades. He usually does not bother completing his homework. He watches television after school until bedtime, he then does his homework when he wakes up in the morning. He once enjoyed playing football for his school but became ineligible due to his grade point average. He does not comply with school attendance rules and in fact presents a truancy problem. Only once, out of the many times Jeremiah has been absent from school, were school staff able to verify that he was at home sick. Jeremiah perceives that teachers and others at his school have labeled him a bad child. He tends to behave or react in ways that align with the perceived labeling. However, Jeremiah has expressed surprise at the school's and the court's stern reaction to his aggressive outburst. Although he disliked the consequences, he accepted them.

The BCD Agency therapist diagnosed Jeremiah with oppositional defiant disorder, with ADHD, and with mood disorder (not otherwise specified). He had been diagnosed with attention deficit disorder (ADD) previously, as a second-grader. His second-grade teacher reported that Jeremiah exhibited behaviors typifying children with ADD; a physician was consulted, who prescribed medication for Jeremiah. Tammy reportedly stopped giving Jeremiah medication when, after two years of his taking the medication, she observed no real behavioral improvement. Jeremiah's self-reports from the Depression Self-Rating Scale and Rosenberg Self-Esteem Scale give some signs of depression and low self-esteem.

Tammy is a permissive parent, lacking firmness in her expectations of Jeremiah. She seldom follows through with promised consequences for behavioral infractions. For example, should Jeremiah refuse to do his chores, Tammy simply does them herself—or asks Alicia to do them. Tammy is preoccupied by Jeremiah's undesirable behavior and has expressed feelings of frustration, helplessness, and stress, all generated by the need to stay watchful concerning Jeremiah's behavior. She sometimes yells at Jeremiah. But when Jeremiah blames Tammy for his problems, attributing them to incompetent parenting on her part, she accepts the blame. Tammy's supervision of Jeremiah is insufficient. School staff reportedly are aware that Jeremiah is on the streets late at night with older teenagers. Two older friends were with Jeremiah at the time he exploded the gasoline and were also present when Jeremiah produced and ignited the M-85. Jeremiah has admitted that on two occasions he exited his house at night to be with friends, without Tammy's knowledge.

Jeremiah and Alicia dislike each other. Alicia describes Jeremiah as mean and disruptive. The two frequently get into physical altercations, fighting or wrestling. In the course of these struggles, they have broken three windows in their house. They have fought using impromptu weapons; for instance, they hit each other using a telephone, leaving Jeremiah with a head wound. Jeremiah also has behaved aggressively toward Alicia's friends. For example, when one friend visited Alicia at home, Jeremiah pushed and injured the friend. Jeremiah has admitted to being aggressive, and he has stated that he often feels a nearly uncontrollable anger. He does not believe this anger is related to any desire to have a father or to any envy of children who do have a father.

Tammy was two years old when her biological parents divorced. Tammy eventually gained a stepfather, who was an alcoholic and a perfectionist. The stepfather verbally and physically abused Tammy and her mother. On one occasion, his abuse of Tammy triggered her mother to call police, and he was subsequently convicted of child abuse and jailed. Tammy completed high school and took some college courses. She has worked since she graduated from high school. She currently works in purchasing for a company near her family's home. The home is a three-bedroom house. It is spacious, comfortably furnished, and clean. Although the family budget is tight, Tammy is able to manage payment of the mortgage and utility bills.

Tammy's mother is quite controlling and often intervenes in Tammy's parenting and other aspects of her life. Reportedly, Tammy once stood up to her mother and followed her own wishes rather than her mother's. The mother's response was to cease all contact with Tammy, Jeremiah, and Alicia. Eighteen months later, Tammy and her mother reconciled. Being cut off by her mother distressed Tammy so much that for a time she obtained some mental health counseling. Tammy makes frequent telephone calls to a stepsister who lives out of state.

2.7.2 Jose

Jose (age 14) broke his brother's nose at home, and his parents filed charges. The judge ordered Jose and his family to enter family counseling services.

Jose and his brother Marco (age 10) often fight over things at home. Each has his own bedroom. Jose does not like Marco get into his room or belongings. He does not like Marco wearing his clothes. He will not allow Marco to wear his clothes even if Marco asks him first. The conflict usually begins with accusations and yelling; then it escalates to shoving and pushing; and finally to punching and kicking. To stop their fights, their parents physically separate them and send them to their rooms. Jose often accuses his parents of playing favorites with of Marco and he runs out of the house. Jose will go home after several hours but he will not reveal where he has been.

Jose drinks beer and liquor with his peers in their homes on weekends. He spends nights at his peers' homes. After drinking with his peers, he often comes home intoxicated. If parents confront him about his drinking, he will become belligerent. In a couple of incidents, he punched holes in the wall of the living room. He also passed out on the sofa several times. His parents have attempted to keep him from seeing his peers. However, he will then sneak out after midnight and not come home until dawn.

Jose has failing grades at school, as well as truancy and insubordination problems. However, he does not engage in any conflict with other students. He does not like school and wants to drop out. His teacher confirmed that he had good grades two years ago. Jose revealed that he has a desire to become a landscaper because in that field he can control his own pace of work. He also revealed that he does not want to become an auto mechanic like his father. He insists that his father should teach Marco, not him, to become a mechanic.

Marco is very polite and responsive in conversation. He revealed that he is afraid of Jose and he does not understand why Jose is so angry at him all the time. He has good grades at school and enjoys math. He has many friends at school and he has won a math contest.

The parents, Toni (age 38) and Maria (age 35), have married for 14 years. After high school, Toni completed his training as an auto mechanic in a technical institute; he has been working in different auto shops or dealerships. Maria completed her cosmetology training and has become a hair stylist since she graduated from high school. The parents sometimes come home late from work and rely on the children to take care of themselves. For two years, both parents have been feeling drifting apart. They have been arguing over many things such as budgeting and parenting. They have not going out by themselves for a year. They have talked about separation but have not made any decision yet; they have not told the children about the possible separation.

2.7.3 McCool Family

Diane (age 16) was arrested after using a telephone to hit her mother's face, bruising her. Her parents filed charges against Diane, and she spent a weekend in a juvenile detention center. After a court hearing, Diane returned home. She and her family were, however, required to attend counseling and receive family services.

Diane's biological parents—Bobby (age 33) and Molly (age 32)—married when she was born. They divorced 12 years ago because Bobby was abusive to Molly. Since the divorce, Bobby has not contacted Diane, nor has he paid child support to Molly. When Diane was six years old, Molly remarried. Diane's stepfather, Zack McCool (age 40), has a son with Molly. The nine-year-old's name is William. Molly works as a manager at a fast-food restaurant.

Molly's parents never abused or neglected her, but they did not show her affection or pay her much attention. She met Bobby in high school and became pregnant with Diane. Her parents were very upset, so Molly moved in with Bobby's family. Molly and Bobby eventually moved to a metropolitan area, and Bobby became abusive to Molly. She was hospitalized several times because he had punched her. However, Molly never filed any charges.

Molly revealed that she and Zack suffered from alcoholism. They had been drinking cases of beer together, becoming intoxicated almost daily, until about three years ago. Then, the couple was involved in a drunk-driving car accident that seriously injured Molly. After the accident, they both attended AA meetings and began to abstain from drinking.

Zack's parents were alcoholics, and they were physically abusive to Zack and his siblings. They spanked them with a belt or wooden spoon, often leaving bruises on their arms and legs. Zack left home as a teenager, dropping out of high school and learning to repair automobiles. He has worked for many years as an auto mechanic. His marriage to Molly is his second marriage. He did not reveal why his first marriage ended. He pays child support to his ex-wife, with whom he has a 17-year-old daughter who visits him regularly.

Diane resents her mother's marriage to Zack and said that Molly and Zack neglect her. She reported that the two used to get drunk almost daily (as indicated by alcohol on breath, slurred speech, staggering gait, passing out). When she was younger, she was often left in the care of neighbors or relatives. But since Molly and Zack became sober, Diane has also felt frustrated and irritated by what she considers their too-close supervision. They reportedly do not like Diane's friends and do not trust her. Diane believes that her mother and stepfather pay more attention to her half-brother William and to each other than to her. Reportedly, they spend more time with William and buy him many things. Diane has complained that Zack has never treated her as a daughter, instead continually criticizing her shortcomings and telling her she cannot do anything right.

Diane and her boyfriend, Nathan (age 16), are sexually active and do not use contraception. She worries that she may be pregnant, and she is afraid to tell Molly. She has been using marijuana since age 12. She, Nathan, and their friends smoke marijuana on a weekly basis. She has also experimented with stimulants in the past. Diane does not like beer and wants to avoid becoming alcoholic like Molly and Zack.

Diane has exhibited poor academic performance (D and F grades) and problem behavior at school. During the current school year, she has been suspended three times; the school has considered expelling her. She has an interest in becoming a hairstylist. She has dyed her hair green and likes to wear spiked collars and chains.

William dislikes Diane because she is mean to him without provocation, yelling at him and calling him names. Reportedly she has never been physically aggressive with him. William feels afraid when Diane and his parents argue. He worries that someone will be hurt in the conflict. William likes school and earns B and C grades. He enjoys playing with his neighbor friends.

2.8 Intimate Partner Violence—Alice and Don

2.8.1 Alice and Don

2.8.1.1 Reason for Referral

CPS substantiated a report that Don (age 13) was being physically abused as well as neglected by his mother, Alice (age 36). Don was placed in a foster home, where he has been residing for two months. The family and foster family have now been referred to First Impact Family Service.

Don reported that when he lives with Alice, she often strikes him and kicks him; she is regularly verbally abusive as well, calling him "asshole," "bastard," or "shithead." Don makes his own meals and has many other chores. Alice admitted that she does hit Don and calls him names. Since Don was placed in foster care, Alice sought counseling at Happy Family Center (HFC). She did not find the counseling to be helpful, and she discontinued the sessions.

2.8.1.2 Alice

Alice's parents had two other daughters and a son, but Alice does not often see her siblings (two of whom are in prison); the four have generally not gotten along well.

Alice's father, Samuel (age 55), died a few years ago; her mother, Maddie (age 51), had divorced him after he was convicted of criminal sexual conduct against one of Alice's sisters and sent to prison. The father had also sexually abused Alice when she was about seven years old, but Alice told no one about that abuse until after her father had died.

When Alice was 10 years old, she and her siblings were placed in foster care because of Maddie's drug use. Eventually, Alice was adopted. In 10th grade, Alice dropped out of school. She has a history of using crack, marijuana, and alcohol.

Alice reportedly worked part-time in fast-food outlets and sporting goods stores while living with Ricky, who later fathered Don. They spent their money on drugs. After Don's birth, Alice and Ricky married. Ricky died of cancer when Don was nine years old. Ricky's parents visited Don and Alice regularly at holiday times, until Alice moved with Don to another state.

Six months before that move, Alice was living with Karl (age 40), who abused her. He repeatedly punched, kicked, and choked her, blacking her eyes, leaving bruises on her arms, and once fracturing her ribs. She obtained emergency room care for the latter injury but did not reveal Karl's abuse to authorities. After beating her, Karl typically apologized for his anger and temper; because of his apologies, she believed Karl loved her. Eventually, on one occasion when Karl choked Alice almost to unconsciousness, Don called the police and Karl was arrested. Alice obtained a restraining order and soon moved away with Don. Reportedly, Karl managed to locate Alice and Don each time they moved away from where he was living. In fact, they moved to three different states fleeing Karl.

Alice reported that Karl was outside her workplace several weeks ago. He approached her, and he reportedly said he loved Alice and hoped she would forgive him for abusing her. He wanted to reconcile and move in with Alice. She told him she would think about it, an answer that reportedly upset him. One week ago, Alice frantically called her social worker because Karl was outside her house and had a shotgun. He left while she was making the call. Although the incident frightened Alice, she did not call police. Later the same day, Karl called her and apologized, crying and asking that they live together again. Alice reported considering the request.

Alice has nightmares and flashbacks concerning Karl's abuse *and* her childhood sexual abuse. She has occasional crying spells that last for hours, grieving over her deceased husband, Ricky. She frequently feels uneasy and unsettled; her hands shake at times. She often uses alcohol to "calm her nerves." Alice consumes five shots of liquor, having blackouts twice a week. She reportedly has not used marijuana or other drugs for a few years.

Currently, Alice is seeking work, using newspaper listings and the state employment office. She has applied for TANF, Medicaid, and unemployment benefits and receives some food from a food pantry.

2.8.1.3 Karl

Karl reported that when he was a child, he received little affection from his father. Karl dropped out of high school. He worked as a security guard for eight years. But after being convicted of car theft, Karl spent three years in prison, following which he could find only odd jobs. Karl denied that he uses any substances. He reported no history of mental health problems in his family of origin.

2.8.1.4 Don

Before Don was placed in foster care, he often overslept on school mornings and rushed to catch his bus. His chores around the house went undone: trash not taken out, dirty dishes in the sink, the cat's litter uncleaned, and his bedroom a mess. He slept too late to wash and groom himself or eat breakfast before school. After school, Don usually watched TV, ignoring homework assignments yet keeping a "C" grade average. He did ask permission to play basketball or go fishing with his friends. He also made a habit of roller-skating inside the house. Don and Alice often had dinner separately. Don went to bed at 11 p.m. He liked football and had posters of cheer-leaders on his bedroom wall.

Don is well-behaved in the foster home. He is polite and cooperative. A psychological evaluation recommended a structured, supportive environment for Don, along with grief counseling regarding his father's death. Don was diagnosed of a learning disability by a school psychologist.

Alice did not witness in Don any desirable or positive behaviors. When Don "talked back" to her or began to walk away from her during confrontations, she yelled at him and slapped or shook him. She was very impatient about Don's undone chores. Alice and Don often argued loudly about the clothes and shoes he wore. She reported that she does not perceive herself as a competent mother and that Don requires parenting from a man. In the past, Karl reportedly had interrupted Alice and Don's exchanges, replacing Alice's instructions to Don with his own instructions. Alice used to agree with Karl's ideas on parenting.

Three months ago, Alice and Don attended a concert. When Don expressed interest in getting the singer's autograph, Alice encouraged him, saying she would go with him to ask for the autograph. Don changed his mind suddenly and Alice began to argue with him. Don then became upset, saying he was going to leave the concert immediately. Alice tried to prevent that by grabbing Don's hands so aggressively that she made red marks in the center of his right palm. Don pulled away but later came back, and Alice and Don remained in their seats until the concert was over.

2.8.1.5 Later Development One

After Don reunited with Alice, she reportedly saw that Karl was hiding behind some bushes across the street and watching her home. Alice suspected that Karl was trying to sneak into her home at night because she heard some funny noise at the door or window at night. She did not know what to do. She was fearful of her life. Don reportedly was putting a knife under his pillow for protection; he claimed that he would cut Karl if Karl broke into their home.

2.8.1.6 Later Development Two

Alice reconciled with Karl and let him move in with her and Don. Alice and Karl made an appointment with a counselor at LMN Counseling Services, but within two months of Karl's moving in, the couple had again broken up; Don attempted to stop the fight between Alice and Karl but Don was thrown to the floor and broke his arm. The result of an altercation ended with a call to police. Karl has not lived in Alice's home since that altercation, and Don has been placed in another foster home, because he was removed from his mother's care in the wake of the call to police.

2.9 Substance Abuse—Kim

2.9.1 *Kim*

Kim (age 25) has three children and has been married for five years to the younger children's father, Leo (age 33). The children are Mark (age 10), Tonya (age 1), and Harry (age 1 month). At Tonya's birth, the infant tested positive for drug exposure. CPS investigated and found Kim to be an abuser of cocaine and alcohol. Kim attended and completed drug treatment, and CPS closed the case. But now Harry has been tested drug-positive at birth, and CPS has recommended a family agency provide services to the family. If the services fail, CPS will remove the children from Kim and Leo's home.

Kim is short and thin and appears tired all the time. She regularly sleeps for 12–15 hours. She pays no attention to her appearance. During the interview with the social worker, her eyes glazed over during their conversation. When Harry cried, she did not pick him up or even look at him. She could not recall the time of his last feeding.

Kim has three older brothers and two older sisters. Although all Kim's siblings live nearby, she has contact with only one sister. Nevertheless, she thought her brothers and other sister would help her if asked to do so. Kim's biological parents, Josh (age 60) and Tina (age 60), divorced six years ago. Since the divorce, Kim sees Josh several times each year. Tina babysits Kim's children several times each month.

Reportedly, when Kim was a child, Josh and Tina abused heroin and alcohol. Kim recalls frequent conflicts and occasional physical altercations between Josh and Tina. Her parents were very strict with their children and did not hesitate to use physical punishment. When Kim was pregnant with Mark, she dropped out of high school. She raised Mark with the support of her parents. When she became an adult, she moved out of the family home, leaving Mark with his grandparents. Kim worked in fast-food restaurants and barely managed a living. Eventually, she got her GED. She had several unsuccessful relationships before meeting Leo.

Leo had served in the Army. He has worked for the post office for many years now and likes his job. He completed high school and earned an associate degree. His parents, Marshall and Lily, were married but Marshall committed suicide when Leo was seven years old and his older brother, Gilbert, was nine years old. Lily (age 61) and remains married to her second husband, Brad (age 60). Brad helped raise Leo and Gilbert. Neither Lily nor Brad has a history of domestic violence, drug abuse, or mental health problems. Leo reported his childhood was happy and his relationship with his stepfather was very loving. Brad and Lily also had a daughter together, Maggie (age 21). Leo, Gilbert, and Maggie always got along well. Although Gilbert and Maggie have moved out of state, they maintain contact with Leo and each other.

Leo revealed that he has seasonal depressive symptoms, for which he has been prescribed psychotherapeutic medication. Leo reportedly has no history of substance abuse. Kim, in contrast, revealed she first used alcohol and marijuana at age 12. She was vague about the frequency of her substance use. She was a social drinker who had used cocaine recreationally. She had completed an outpatient drug treatment. However, she could not name any effective method of preventing relapse and was vague about when she had last used alcohol or cocaine.

Kim showed little interest in further drug treatment, saying it would conflict with work and childcare. Leo was very concerned about the children's well-being. He believed that Kim was not addicted to cocaine or alcohol but was being influenced by her sister to "party." Leo was very supportive of Kim's getting treatment, but he also stated that the decision to pursue it belonged to Kim. He was uncertain, moreover, about requiring drug screening for Kim. He needs Kim to be available to care for the children in their home. Leo and Kim reportedly discipline the children with solely non-physical methods.

Mark and Tonya appear healthy and active. Mark shows good bonding and affection with Leo. Kim appears to keep the children at an emotional distance. Mark earns B grades at school and enjoys playing basketball with friends after school. Mark also likes to play racing video games.

Kim and Leo have a good marital relationship, with no history of domestic violence. Many of the couple's friends are Leo's coworkers. Leo was raised a Catholic, but the couple does not attend church. Leo's income is sufficient for the family; the mortgage on their house is nearly paid and they own two cars (one for Leo, one for Kim).

2.10 Homelessness—Brianna; Lorraine

2.10.1 Brianna

Brianna (age 28) and her four children (age 7, 8, 9, and 10) were staying in a shelter. CPS referred this family to EFG family preservation services.

Brianna recently lost her telemarketing job and the family was evicted from their apartment. Brianna has abused crack cocaine and alcohol for several years. She missed so many workdays that she was fired. Before she was fired, she spent most of her income on the substances and did not pay her bills. Before they were evicted, there was little food in their apartment and the utilities were not functional. When she was evicted, the family lost all their furniture and most of their belongings.

Brianna had not received any drug treatment in the past. She understood that her substance abuse had ruined her family life. She worried about whether she could make it.

Brianna wanted to leave the shelter as soon as possible. Her children (two boys and two girls) became restless when they spent too much time indoors. The older ones fought with other children in the shelter. The younger ones were not happy because they were teased by other children in school for their old and worn clothes.

Brianna's mother was living in the next town but could not take them in because of limited space. Brianna's cousin John and his family lived several blocks from her former apartment. Both Brianna's mother and cousin had helped her out of crises (e.g., food shortage, bills, etc.) in the past, but they were now very frustrated because she continued her substance use.

Brianna claimed that her children's behavior was fine and she did not use any physical punishment. She insisted that she never used substances in front of the children. She could only vaguely recall their academic performance at school.

2.10.2 Lorraine

Lorraine (age 35) and her children—Albert (age 15), Kristy (age 13), Perry (age 7), and Dora (age 4)—are homeless after being evicted recently from their former address. Lorraine recently lost her job, and the family has no income or food. Most of their belongings were stolen when the evicting landlords placed the items outdoors when the family was away; only some clothes were left undisturbed. CPS investigated and referred the family to RST family agency.

Lorraine has been in substance abuse treatment for alcohol and crack cocaine abuse, but the loss of her job means that she will have to discontinue it. A therapist at Project Will confirmed that Lorraine has actively participated in a support group. Lorraine has positive experience in the support group, despite being excluded from one meeting 10 days ago because she arrived late. Her tardiness was due to a medical appointment (tests for headache symptoms) at Good Heart Hospital. Excluded from the meeting, Lorraine nevertheless listened to the session from outside the door.

Last week Lorraine completed a drug screen that yielded a positive result for opiates. She said that she had taken headache medication, possibly containing morphine, prescribed by a Good Heart Hospital emergency room physician. However, she could not specify the visit's exact date. Furthermore, yesterday Lorraine refused to provide a urine specimen at Project Will; she reportedly was short of time because she needed to pick Perry up at school. Lorraine also refuses to complete urine drop tests at Fine Lab facilities because they gave her positive results.

Lorraine has become increasingly hostile toward the RST social worker. She has stated that she will take her children and leave the city. She rejects inpatient treatment, saying there is no one she trusts to care for her children. She needs more time to prove her ongoing success in Project Will.

Lorraine has been receiving therapy for posttraumatic stress disorder (PTSD) at Comfort Clinic, but she will have to discontinue it now that she lacks an income. Reportedly, she experiences flashback episodes of childhood sexual abuse. Lorraine has called her mother concerning the childhood abuse Lorraine experienced; her mother reportedly apologized to her, and Lorraine believes that she "found some answers" during this call to her mother. Lorraine also reported that the perpetrator of her sexual abuse, who is her uncle, has attempted to talk with her.

At the Good Heart Hospital visit prior to 10 days ago, Lorraine was found to be suffering from ringworm all over her body. The condition being highly contagious, she was advised by a hospital physician to stay at home for a week. She had no money for the prescribed medication. During this time, Lorraine's daughter Kristy took on the care of her two younger siblings at home, hoping they would not contract ringworm. Three days later Kristy also showed signs of the fungus herself. A pediatrician found a high level of lead in Dora's blood.

Kristy, Perry, and Dora appear age-appropriate in their development and behaviors. Kristy and Perry enjoy school, typically earning B's. The children appear to get along well, and Kristy tends to help her younger siblings consistently. The current crisis appears, however, to worry Kristy and Perry. Perry has expressed sadness over his lost toys and other belongings.

Since the eviction, Albert has stayed with a family friend Betty. Lorraine has complained that Betty is preventing Lorraine from contacting Albert. Although Albert likes his mother to visit him at Betty's, he does not want to leave Betty's home to go with Lorraine, for fear Lorraine may ultimately abandon him. Albert and Betty both have reported that, a year ago, Lorraine struck Albert with her fist. However, CPS found no record of Albert suffering physical abuse.

The children's fathers have paid no child support to Lorraine, and the fathers' whereabouts are unknown. Lorraine's mother lives in another state.

2.11 Illness—Ida

2.11.1 Ida

Ida (age 38) is a widow. She married her first husband, Brock, when she was 17 years old. Ida divorced Brock because of domestic violence. Ida and Brock had no children. About 10 years ago, Ida married Keith. They had two children, Kyle (age 9) and Kelly (age 8). Keith died three years ago. On his deathbed, Keith revealed to Ida that he had AIDS. After Keith died, Ida's physician confirmed that she was HIV-positive. About two years after Keith's death, her health deteriorated. She was hospitalized several times, and she lost her job and health insurance.

Ida appears older than her age, with gray hair and wrinkles. She complains that her knees and fingers are painful. She has also shown depressive symptoms and abused alcohol. She met Keith at an Alcohol Anonymous meeting. After they married, Ida became sober. After Keith passed away and she was diagnosed with HIV, she became very angry and sad. She resumed drinking. Her drinking became heavier as her health deteriorated, reaching a point at which she consumed a 40-ounce bottle of beer or six shots of liquor each day. She is now intoxicated almost every day, and she has had several blackouts in the previous 12 months. She has crying spells and cannot sleep at night. She thinks of Keith and worries about herself and her children. She has no suicidal ideation.

Ida does not comply with her medication, complaining about their side effects. While her physician confirms that the medication will maintain her health, she believes that she will die prematurely anyway. Unable to function at work, Ida was fired. She has been unable to take care of her children. Her children and home became filthy, and the children's school filed a report. CPS investigated and substantiated the report. CPS provided case management that helped the family obtain benefits from TANF and Medicaid. The family has been living in an apartment with Section 8 housing benefits.

Kyle and Kelly appear to exhibit age-appropriate development. They are active and follow Ida's instructions. They know that Ida is sick but are unaware of her exact diagnosis. Ida has not revealed it to them and will not allow them to be tested for HIV. Staff and the children's school and the family's church are also unaware of Ida's HIV status, because she fears prejudice against the family.

Their teachers have reported that Kyle and Kelly are good students and get along with other students. But a rumor has been circulated that they are sick, and some troublemakers have picked on them. Recently, too, the family's church has rejected their participation, not explaining why. Ida suspects that her medical condition has somehow become known to church members. Kyle and Kelly enjoy playing with neighbor children.

Their paternal grandparents have visited Kyle and Kelly weekly, and they took care of the two while Ida was hospitalized. They have expressed guilty feelings about Ida's medical condition. They have also worried about the children's living and health conditions. While on the one hand Ida appreciates their help, it also upsets her, worrying that they may want to take Kelly and Kyle away from her. Ida's own parents and other relatives have had no physical contact with her since finding out she is HIV-positive. Her parents do call Ida and have sent money at the holidays.

2.12 Kinship Care—DJ; Jim and Lana

2.12.1 DJ

2.12.1.1 Reason for Involvement

This family came to the attention of CPS one year ago, when the children were physically abused by the mother's boyfriend and were subsequently removed into foster care. Two months ago, the children were returned to their mother. She has failed to bring DJ for psychotherapy at an outpatient mental health clinic as recommended by his physician at the county hospital where he was treated for broken bones resulting from the abuse. For that reason, CPS again removed DJ from his mother's care two weeks ago, and CPS placed DJ in the care of his aunt, Julie.

2.12.1.2 Family Composition

Mother:	Mandy (age 31)
Fathers:	Jorge (father of DJ): Unknown address
	Damon (father of James and Verna): Known address
	John (father of Howard): Known address
Children:	Howard (age 13)
	DJ (age 11)
	James (age 5)
	Verna (age 3)
Significant Others:	
	Julie (aunt of DJ)

2.12.1.3 Family History

Two months ago, when the children were returned to the mother, the family moved across the city. The family is residing in a two-bedroom apartment. The children have transferred to schools in the new neighborhood. The family receives food stamps.

2.12.1.4 Parent's History

Mandy and her four siblings were raised by their parents, responsible people who did not abuse or neglect their children. Both of Mandy's parents died about five years ago. Because her parents moved their family here from the Midwest before Mandy could complete 12th grade, she has no high school diploma. Since leaving school, she has worked for many different part-time jobs.

Mandy is a single mother of four. She reportedly has no contact with the father of DJ. Damon, the father of James and Verna, sometimes drops in on Mandy and the children and gives them cash (typically $20). At one point, Mandy held two jobs. She currently works six days a week from 2 to 11 p.m. for an inn. She sometimes works double shifts, trying to earn enough to cover the family's expenses. She typically appears tired, if not exhausted. When Mandy goes to work, she employs a reliable babysitter for James and Verna. On occasion, James and Verna stay overnight with their paternal grandmother.

Mandy has complained that DJ is moody, even unstable, and easily enraged. While DJ has told Mandy that he loves her, he has also threatened to kill her. Moreover, he has thrown his younger siblings to the floor as a means of expressing his displeasure at having to live with Mandy. Mandy reported that she has tried hard to maintain a good relationship with DJ; however, she was unable to provide any examples of her efforts in this regard. Mandy believes that DJ likes staying with Julie because Julie indulges DJ, permitting him activities and buying him things that Mandy would not. Mandy has not recently contacted Julie, whom she labeled a "welfare queen."

Following DJ's most recent removal, Mandy was upset by the CPS's action; she reluctantly agreed to in-home counseling but nevertheless balked at arranging for DJ to complete the recommended clinic-based psychotherapy. Her busy schedule reportedly would not accommodate psychotherapy appointments. She does not believe that DJ has mental health problems requiring therapy or medication; he is just a difficult child to her.

Since Mandy wants DJ to return to the family home, she is willing to take DJ for psychotherapy appointments, but not at the clinic recommended for him by his hospital physician. She feels tired after years of struggle with DJ and she feels disappointed by the outcomes of earlier interventions. She doubts whether DJ's behavior and relationships with his family members will be improved.

Mandy's apartment has been without heat since the family moved in two months ago. Her rent has been paid on time, but the landlord has denied gas company representatives access to the basement to turn on the gas. The social worker offered to speak with the landlord, but Mandy said she preferred to handle the matter herself.

Mandy reported having no history of substance use or mental health problems. She does not know the history of substance use and mental health problems among her children's paternal relatives.

2.12.1.5 History of Children Not in Placement

Howard appears well-fed and adequately clothed. He dresses in black clothing and wears a metal-spiked choker. He avoids eye and seems uninterested in conversation. Although Howard and DJ reportedly sometimes argue, Howard claims that he understands DJ's moodiness.

Howard attends middle school and he dislikes his new school and its teachers; he tends to earn C grades. His favorite subject is physical education and he wants to attend Peace High School because he likes its basketball team. He likes going out with his friends (most of whom are in his class at school) in his free time. He sometimes is with them away from home until after 11 p.m. and Mandy asks no questions about it. Howard was vague regarding his whereabouts and activities at such times; he was very vague about his experience with substance use. Howard reportedly does not help with household chores or supervision of his younger siblings.

James appears well-fed and adequately clothed. No marks or bruises can be observed on his person. He needs a great deal of attention from Mandy. James dislikes DJ because DJ gets angry at him easily and yells at or hits him. James often spends time watching television alone.

Verna appears well-fed and adequately clothed. No marks or bruises can be observed on her person. Verna demonstrates age-appropriate behaviors including a great deal of activity generally and attempts to get hold of any object within her reach. She wants affection from her mother, trying to cling to Mandy. Verna has a few old dolls with which she sometimes plays alone.

2.12.1.6 History of Child in Placement

DJ appears well-fed and adequately clothed. He is jittery and maintains poor eye contact. DJ currently attends Goodbridge School, the neighborhood school in his aunt Julie's neighborhood. He was placed in Julie's care following a second removal from his mother's care. DJ said he likes the school and its teachers. He tends to make C grades.

DJ said that he frequently argued with Mandy, attributing to his distaste for chores in Mandy's home. He did not like Mandy's nagging him about chores in front of his friends. He wanted Mandy to give him more money to spend.

DJ reported that Mandy often left him, James, and Verna alone at night. He had sometimes hit the younger siblings with his hand and with a belt for doing something wrong (e.g., being noisy, not sitting down when told to, jumping on the bed, and fighting). He hit them in a manner that did not really hurt them. When his mother was home, he did not hit them at all. DJ denied any substance use. He denied having threatened to kill Mandy and to jump out of a window (Howard confirmed that the latter reported threat had been a joke on DJ's part).

DJ enjoys staying with Julie because she gave him a dog, a bicycle, clothes, and toys. Julie helps him with homework, makes him laugh, and plays video games with him. DJ also gets along with Julie's children.

A year ago, DJ was hospitalized for five days with fractured ribs and a broken leg resulting from physical abuse at the hands of Mandy's then-boyfriend. DJ's mental health was also assessed in the hospital, and he was diagnosed with exposure to domestic violence by history, impulse control disorder not otherwise specified, and bipolar I disorder. A physician recommended DJ begin individual psychotherapy immediately. While living in foster care, DJ had a manic episode requiring 10 days' hospitalization. From the time of his hospitalization until he was returned to his mother, DJ took medication prescribed for his mental illness and he also attended outpatient therapy.

2.12.2 Jim and Lana

Jim (age 70) and Lana (age 68) adopted seven children of their daughters'. One of these daughters died from an overdose of cocaine. One daughter disappeared and left her children to them. Jim and Lana also adopted the children of the youngest daughter, who abused them. The oldest grandchild is 16 years old and the youngest is seven years old. Both Jim and Lana are retired and they rely on their monthly Social Security as their only income. This income is just enough for the rent of a house and utilities, but their meager finances cannot cover care of the adopted grandchildren.

Since the grandchildren were adopted, Lana has forgone regular physical examinations. Currently she is not taking any prescription medications; she does not use any substances.

Lana often cries at night with grief over her late daughter. Lana cries so hard that she cannot fall asleep. Since her late daughter moved out of state, it took a long time to find and visit her dying daughter. Lana witnessed her late daughter's pain and suffering in the dying bed. She often thinks of her late daughter's suffering and blames herself. Lana believes that she might be able to save her late daughter if she could find her soon enough. She worries about the daughter who disappeared two years ago. Lana often feels fatigue and complains about headache.

Jim's joints act up so badly that he can hardly walk around or move his arms. He cannot afford medication and he was denied participation in the Senior Pharmacy Program.

The four-bedroom house is an increasingly messy, chaotic environment. Some of the grandchildren are hyperactive, and their occasional destructive behavior has damaged the rental house. Several walls show dents and holes caused by punching and throwing objects. Two bedrooms' doors were kicked in as the grandchildren fought over clothing and other belongings. The older grandchildren complain that the younger ones disturb their things.

The kitchen sink is routinely full of dirty dishes, and food waste can be found scattered on the floor. Cockroaches have been observed in the kitchen sink area, while empty beer cans (two of them) were found under the sofa and cigarette butts were found littering the house's backdoor entrance. A strong odor has begun coming from the basement, which grandparents have not entered in over six months. CPS has investigated and recommended that the grandparents clean the house immediately. What's more, their landlord has threatened to evict the family.

2.12.2.1 Later Development

Four months later, Jim died of a heart attack.

At night, Lana often cries with grief over her late husband. She believes Jim might still be alive if he had consulted physicians and purchased needed medications. Lana's crying often leaves her unable to fall asleep. In daylight hours, too, she often cries over Jim when attempting to speak of him, becoming unable to maintain a conversation. She feels helpless and lonely. She feels she has nothing to look forward to. Several times in the past month, she has "seen" Jim late at night, sitting on his favorite sofa in their home.

Over the weekend, Lana's grandson Justice (age 16) was charged with vandalism and sent to a juvenile detention center. He has just returned home and is waiting for his court hearing.

2.13 Foster Care and Aging Out—Dorie

2.13.1 Dorie

Dorie (age 18) was removed from biological mother because she was sexually abused by biologial mother's live-in boyfriend. Biological mother accused that Dorie was lying about the abuse and refused to keep live-in boyfriend out. Parental rights were terminated and no relatives were identified as reliable caregivers. Dorie has been in foster care for nine years and she rejected adoption.

Dorie is currently living with a foster mother. Dorie is attending high school and is doing very well according to the teacher/principal. Dorie has no current mental or physical diagnosis, and she is not prescribed any medications. Dorie has an intern work placement from school at a senior center where Dorie files records and does other clerical duties. Dorie is very well liked in the senior center and in the school. She is polite and respectful to others and staff. She gets along with other students and plays drum in the school band.

Dorie appears to be capable of being independent in the next two years. At this time, Dorie needs supervision and care. Dorie wishes to get a certificate from a postsecondary (or vocational) school, and she has a desire to become a songwriter or veterinarian. Dorie does not know how to cook but she takes care of personal hygiene. However, Dorie is not able to identify other skills required for her independent living in the future. Dorie hopes that she can continue to live with the foster mother in the future. Dorie's foster mother has assisted Dorie in becoming as functional emotionally and physically as Dorie is at the present time. The foster mother will continue to support Dorie in becoming independent; however, the foster mother has no concrete plan that how long Dorie can live with her.

Dorie completed a psychiatric evaluation last year with very favorable remarks from the psychiatrist. According to the evaluation, Dorie is pleasant, positive and engages in conversation about life. The psychiatrist noted that there needs to be some attention paid to Dorie's goals as to Dorie's capabilities. Dorie functions very well with some safeguards built in. In the past, Dorie had engaged in self-destructive and disruptive behaviors as well as inappropriate relationships due to childhood experiences with men. For instance, she has superficial cuts or deep scratches on her wrists. She once was easily agitated and had frequent outbursts in class. She had several boyfriends in the past and she performed oral sex on them; she however denies any sexual intercourse. She had changed five foster homes because of her disruptive and sexual behaviors. Currently, Dorie well behaves and is not sexually active and has no boyfriend. Dorie attends school regularly, turns in homework assignments on time, completes intern placement at work, and intends to graduate from high school. Her self-esteem appears to be fine. Dorie gets along with peers and enjoys activities with them. The only concern is that Dorie is 30 pounds over the desirable weight at her age, according to her family physician.

Dorie's foster mother is credited for Dorie's significant improvement. Dorie has changed her behaviors and becomes responsible and positive since she has been living with the current foster mother. Dorie has learned how to clean personal living area. She has more positive outlooks to herself. She understands that her self-destructive and disruptive behaviors are attention or affection seeking. Reportedly, she receives unconditional and nonjudgmental affection from the current foster mother. Dorie successfully replaces her undesirable behaviors with responsible behaviors at home and school.

There are different opinions about Dorie's capabilities. The teacher/principal states that Dorie's grades are B's, except a C in math. On the contrary, the foster mother states that Dorie cannot read and comprehend even basic information. Moreover, there is a disagreement between CPS and the foster care agency on the intermediate goals for Dorie. The foster care agency and foster mother are very cautious, whereas CPS as well as school are rather optimistic that Dorie will be ready for the adult world herself. The mixed messages do confuse Dorie's vision of future. Nevertheless, there is no clear and agreeable plan for Dorie's future.

2.14 Residential Care—Mike

2.14.1 Mike

About 16 months ago, Mike (age 12) was found performing sexualized behavior on a neighbor child at home. Later, his mother caught him molesting his stepbrother (age 6). His mother and stepfather reported the incident to CPS. After investigation and substantiation, Mike was removed from home and eventually was placed in a boys' home. In the group home, he revealed that he was sexually molested by a babysitter when he was eight years old. He had molested his stepbrother over a period of one year. In the group home, he successfully completed his psychotherapy and has made satisfactory progress. He reportedly got along with other children in the boys' home and exhibited appropriate behavior. CPS considered reunification between Mike and his family. CPS referred Mike and his family to HIJ family preservation services.

Mike's parents divorced when he was very young. Although he was in his mother's custody, he frequently visited with his father. He had a close relationship with his father. His mother remarried and Mike continued to live with his mother and stepfather. Mike's parents remained friends but lived in different towns.

Mike's mother, stepfather, and stepbrother were living in a small two-bedroom house. The house had an unfinished storm cellar. His mother and stepfather occupied one bedroom and the stepbrother occupied the other bedroom. Both mother and stepfather were employed. Their family was barely financially sufficient. Maternal grandparents were supportive in babysitting their step-grandchildren. Mother and stepfather were glad that Mike might reunite with them, but they wonder if Mike's father might try to take Mike.

Mike's father never remarried and lived alone in a one-bedroom trailer. He was a maintenance worker in a factory. He liked to hunt and owned firearms (a pistol and a hunting rifle). Mike's father was glad that Mike might reunite with him, but he wondered if the mother might take Mike. There were young children who lived in the trailer park.

2.15 Reunification—Cindy; Shawn

2.15.1 Cindy

Cindy (age 9) and her brother Thomas (age 12) were removed from their home one year ago because they had multiple marks and bruises on their arms, legs, and backs. Reportedly their mother used a belt to punish them for their unruly behavior. Cindy reported that she and Thomas performed sexualized behavior at home. Cindy later was silent about the allegation and Thomas denied it. While Cindy was placed in a foster home and showed stabilized behavior, Thomas had behavior problems when he spent time in several other foster homes. Mother had completed parenting classes. CPS considered reunification between Cindy and her family. The parents agreed that the family preservation services conduct the reunification process.

Cindy had mixed feelings about to the potential reunification. She recalled her trauma of being physically punished by her parents in the past. She was also fearful that Thomas would be there if she reunited with her family. She refused to talk about why she was fearful of Thomas. She appeared to enjoy her life in the foster home and expressed her desire to be adopted by her foster parents. Her parents had missed many visitation appointments with Cindy, but they had maintained regular visitation with Thomas.

Cindy's parents and two other sons (age 7 and 10) were living in a three-bedroom apartment. Parents occupied one bedroom and each son occupied another bedroom. Father was a hard-working mechanic, and mother was a housewife and was active in church activities. Parents believed that Cindy lied about the allegation of sexualized behavior, because she had often lied in the past. Reportedly, Cindy had difficulty following parental instructions and talked back to them, and Cindy sometimes was aggressive toward the other children. They blamed Cindy for breaking up the family. Their excuses of sporadic visitation with Cindy were that they did not have enough time to visit two children in two different towns. They were disappointed that Thomas was not returning home. Reunification with Cindy would be a steppingstone for their reunification with Thomas.

The two brothers at home missed Cindy and Thomas. They expressed willingness to share one bedroom so that Cindy would have her own room.

2.15.1.1 Later Development

The parents decided to relinquish their parental rights concerning Cindy, but they wanted to reunite with Thomas. They refused to let Cindy know of this decision themselves. Instead, the parents insisted that Cindy should hear the news from the family preservation worker. When she was told what her parents had decided, Cindy was shocked and saddened. Upon learning of the parents' choice, CPS sought the family preservation worker's recommendations about next steps to take.

2.15.2 Shawn

Lisa (age 30) and Tim (age 40) had been living together for 10 years, and Shawn (age 7) was their only child. Lisa was perceived as a slow learner in high school and she passed away last year. Tim was diagnosed with paranoia schizophrenia. After the death of Lisa, school officials began to complain that Tim could not take care of Shawn. Since Tim could not maintain a stable job, he and Shawn became homeless. Six months ago, the CPS removed Shawn from Tim's care and placed Shawn in his paternal grandmother's care. Tim attended recommended psychiatric services at a local mental health clinic, and with the help of CPS, Tim had been living in an apartment. One month ago, Shawn was returned to Tim's care. The family was still under the supervision of the court. Tim's paternal grandmother, Pam, visited Tim and Shawn weekly.

Reportedly, Shawn refused to follow Tim's instructions and had daily temper tantrums. Tim argued with Shawn about his daily routine (e.g., brushing teeth, bathing, and eating meals). Since Tim strongly believed that Pam had "spoiled" Shawn, Tim had considered stopping visitations between Shawn and Pam. Worrying about potential bad influence from neighbors, Tim did not like Shawn to play with the neighbor children.

Shawn worried and felt sad most of the time. He did not share his feelings with Tim. Reportedly, Tim did not play with him. Shawn watched TV at home alone while Tim did the housekeeping chores. Shawn felt bad because he did not do a good job with his chores (laundry and cleaning dishes). Shawn wanted to again live with Pam. Shawn showed some signs of language delays and he felt that other students were better than he was. At night, Shawn "saw" toys running around in his bedroom and he had difficulty of falling asleep.

Tim had visual and audio hallucinations. Tim had illusions that spiders crawled on his arms. Tim reported that the toilet at home talked to him. Tim was very vague about his compliance with the prescribed psychotherapeutic medication. Tim complained that former therapists did not support him and accused him being a bad parent.

2.16 Adoption—Ike

2.16.1 Ike

Ike (age 16) was referred to this family service agency with the expectation that a foster home (and potentially adoptive family) would be located for him.

Ike's parents were post office employees. Both parents used marijuana and cocaine, and both abused Ike. If Ike balked at doing chores or failed to do them properly, his father hit Ike with his fists, leaving bruises. Ike's mother became agitated easily and yelled at Ike frequently. Once she threw a frying pan at Ike, barely missing him.

When Ike was 13 years old, his parents' physical abuse led to his removal from the home. He spent three months in a foster home. During that time, Ike's parents reportedly completed parenting classes and produced negative drug screens. Both parents also attended a substance abuse treatment program. Ike was thus returned to his parents. Two months later, his father assaulted Ike and broke his ribs, after Ike came in one night intoxicated. About the incident, Ike's mother claimed that Ike provoked his father and deserved punishment. This time, Ike and his younger brother Barry were both removed from the parents' home and placed in a foster home. Both parents had tested positive for marijuana and cocaine, they had failed to complete their substance abuse treatment, and they refused to take further parenting classes. Some two years later, a court terminated their parental rights. At the time of the boys' second removal, none of the relatives showed interest in taking Ike and Barry in.

When living in his parents' home, Ike had used alcohol and marijuana. He sometimes sneaked away from the house to join peers in getting intoxicated. Ike disliked his parents, and substance use helped him manage his fear of his parents. Ike experiences flashbacks and nightmares concerning the trauma inflicted on him in his parents' home. When Ike was removed to foster home for the first time, he briefly received counseling, but he did not freely share his deepest concerns with his counselor.

After the second removal, Ike expressed a desire to reunite with his parents. In court, the parents said that they did not want Ike in their home because he was incorrigible. Following the second removal, Ike expressed feelings of anger, sadness, and hopelessness. His foster parents noticed and resented Ike's increasing argumentativeness, even belligerence. He also picked fights at school and was discovered drinking with a group of neighborhood teenagers. A year after the second removal, Ike had changed foster homes several times (meanwhile, Barry remained in the first foster home).

Considering Ike's substance abuse, disruptive behavior, and tendency toward violence, CPS found an opening for him in a residential facility Open Place. Initially,

Ike reportedly found it difficult to adjust to this new, rather restrictive environment. He often disrupted structured activities at Open Place and violated its rules.

Following the court's termination of his mother and father's parental rights, however, Ike began to get along much better at Open Place. His grades also have been steadily improving. He completed substance abuse treatment successfully and has earned incentives and privileges Open Place offers its residents to reward success. Ike regularly attends therapy, addressing his trauma and emotional fallout. He has complied with his doctor's prescription of medications. Ike's therapist and the Open Place house parent confirm the desirable change in his behavior. He is respectful and gets along with peers. Ike has also been participating in an independent living program.

Ike has stated that he wants to attend community college or college, perhaps to become an electrician. (When he was a young child, he enjoyed dismantling and reassembling small appliances, an activity that reportedly angered his parents.) Ike has already identified several community colleges with technical majors of interest to him, but he worries about the financial cost of pursuing his goal.

Ike has no wish to be reunited with his biological parents or their relatives. He enjoys calling Barry. Ike is ambivalent about the idea of adoption.

2.16.1.1 Later Development

The social worker introduced Ike to Mr. and Mrs. Jones and subsequently arranged for Ike to spend several weekends visiting their home, which they had opened to foster children. Ike demonstrated maturity and responsibility during those visits; he and Mr. and Mrs. Jones appeared to respect each other. Two months after they were brought together, Ike was placed with the Joneses, an arrangement that has made both Ike and the foster parents happy. Indeed, Mr. and Mrs. Jones plan to adopt Ike.

Ike recognizes that in the Jones' home, he enjoys more freedom and benefits from the kind of care inherent in a natural family environment. Using information obtained for him by his foster parents, he has devised an education plan that involves adding electrician classes to his regular schooling. Furthermore, Mr. Jones' work in building maintenance will provide Ike with opportunities for hands-on experiences in electrical work.

3 Case Examples in Children and Family Outpatient Services

3.1 Depression—Eli; Greta; Quenton

3.1.1 *Eli*

His father referred Eli (age 15) to a mental health outpatient clinic, but Eli remains unable to identify any reason of his own to seek mental health care. Eli's intake session resulted in a diagnosis of adjustment disorder with mixed anxiety and depressed mood. Since receiving the diagnosis, he has attended weekly therapy sessions.

Eli's biological parents—Ben (age 40) and Rosie (age 35)—were married for 16 years and had three children, Eli, Kimberly (age 10), and Toni (age 8). When Eli was 12 years old, his parents separated and then divorce last year. Ben accused Rosie of beginning an extramarital affair with Frank (age 34), her current live-in boyfriend, before officially separating from Ben. Ben has complained that Rosie stole money from him and spent it on Frank. Rosie obtained a restraining order against Ben because of his prior domestic violence conviction. Ben has reportedly attempted suicide in the past and been hospitalized to treat manic depression.

When Ben and Rosie separated, Rosie retained custody of the children. Two years ago, Rosie allegedly hit Eli with a wooden spoon, punishment that left bruises. Frank allegedly beat Eli but Rosie did not intervene. Child Protective Services (CPS) investigated but did not substantiate either instance of alleged maltreatment.

When his parents divorced, the court granted Eli's wish to live with Ben (Kimberly and Toni live with Rosie). Ben and Rosie's conflict has continued subsequently even to their divorce, and Rosie's visitation with Eli has not gone smoothly. The parents accuse each other of defying the court's visitation order, and they disagree about child support. Until 10 months ago, Ben was complying with court orders by driving Eli to North City (500 miles away) every other week for visits with Rosie. However, Eli tired of Rosie's (and her relatives') criticisms of Ben, so much so that Eli refused further visitation. As a result, for six months Rosie and Eli only spoke by telephone, every two weeks; Rosie placed the calls.

Then, four months ago Eli resumed his trips to North City, at Ben's insistence. Rosie's behavior in Eli's presence became confrontational. Three months ago, according to Eli and Ben, Rosie and her mother came unannounced to Ben's home (which is also his parents' home) to see Eli; the two allegedly tried to force Eli into their car, and a struggle ensued that ended with involvement of the police (Ben's mother saw the struggle and called the police). For a second time, Eli refused further visits with Rosie.

DOI: 10.4324/9781003316688-3

Eli's therapist arranged for a family mediation meeting three weeks ago; Rosie and Frank arrived at the scheduled time. Ben and Eli arrived shortly afterward, but learning of Frank's presence, Ben and Eli refused to attend and left. Rosie refused to meet with the therapist without Frank. Thus family mediation (as well as joint counseling for Rosie and Eli) is impossible. Rosie and Eli have not seen each other since the failed mediation session; Eli's court-ordered summer visit of six to eight weeks in North City looms.

Ben, Eli, and Eli's paternal grandparents reside together in a rural area; the grandparents operate a small-scale horse ranch. The grandfather (age 62) and Ben are union workers at an automobile plant. Rosie is a paralegal with a law firm. Frank is an auto insurance agent. There is no history of substance abuse or mental illness in Ben's or in Rosie's family.

Eli obtains little emotional support from Ben; they spend almost no quality time together, and Eli does not share his thoughts or feelings with Ben. Eli enjoys camping, fishing, working with ranch, and television. He engages in these activities with Ben's father. On the other hand, Eli has a frustrating relationship with Ben's mother, whose health problems include epilepsy and who uses an oxygen tank. Eli gets irritated easily by his grandmother's demands such as making coffee and heating soup for her. Eli generally appears to experience the kind of mood swings common to teenagers and to share their typical disdain for rules and chores (except for working with ranch). He is not aggressive or argumentative and has never run away, even for a few hours. Ben gives Eli an allowance as an incentive for completing chores. Although Ben has recently accompanied Eli to some dirt-bike races and social activities, Ben still describes Eli as withdrawn, depressive, and angry.

Eli does show signs of depressive mood and anxiety, although he is free of night-mares, flashbacks, hallucinations, or suicidal/homicidal ideation. His appetite is good; he cannot fall asleep before midnight on most nights. He becomes sad thinking of Rosie, and he does want to talk to Rosie by telephone. However, when Eli does speak with Rosie by phone, he is moody and irritable afterward, often complaining of a headache. After a call from Rosie, he goes to his room where he cuts pictures into pieces or listens to music to unwind and feel better.

Eli also feels fear and anxiety concerning Rosie. He refuses to return to North City, no matter what the consequences of refusal are; he says that Ben has no influence on his refusal. Eli is preoccupied by thoughts of threats Rosie allegedly made to rob or burn down Ben's home and shoot Ben's family's horses. Eli perceives her threats as genuine. Eli is preoccupied by ongoing thoughts concerning the "abusive" incidents that prompted the initial CPS investigation. He expressed strong distaste for affec-tionate contact with Rosie or Frank. Moreover, he fears that Rosie will coerce him concerning summer visitation. Eli has claimed that he would kill Rosie by any available means if she attempted by force to bring him to North City. Reportedly, Eli has no actual homicidal or suicidal plan.

Eli has few friends, and no one his age lives in his rural neighborhood. When he is with peers, he typically experiences low self-esteem. Results for the peer subscale of the Hare Self-Esteem Scale suggest that he has low self-esteem when among peers. About 10 months ago, while in the company of a 10-year-old neighbor, Eli played with matches and caused a fire in nearby woods. He was able to extinguish it using water and dirt. Eli tends not to treat the animals on the ranch with humanity. He has repeatedly chased the horses while riding a four-wheeler, and he throws rocks at cats.

Despite testing at a fourth-grade level in reading, Eli typically earns B grades in school and has not failed any subjects. He gets along with teachers and fellow students. He has never been involved in a school fight and has never been suspended. Once a student did call him names, but Eli simply ignored the remarks and walked away from the student. He reportedly has never used alcohol or drugs.

3.1.2 Greta

Greta (age 14) and Sylvia (age 11) were removed from their parents to foster care amid allegations of physical and sexual abuse perpetrated against them by the father. After five months in placement, they are in their third foster home. Their father's sexual abuse of Sylvia has been substantiated, and CPS has prohibited Greta and Sylvia's visitation with their parents. Drug tests showed that the father was positive for marijuana use and the mother was positive for cocaine use.

Greta reported the initial alleged abuse to CPS, and she feels guilty over the separation from parents. Both parents have blamed Greta for the separation and their other trouble with authorities.

Greta has depressive mood, and she frequently experiences 30-minute crying spells, both at bedtime and during the day. The removal angered her; she worries that she and her sister will never reunite with their parents. Greta has difficulty falling asleep and she has nightmares. Her appetite is poor, and she is often fatigued or suffering from headache. She is no longer interested in playing her flute, which she once enjoyed doing. Greta does not get along with her younger sister, arguing with Sylvia frequently and occasionally expressing her impatience with her by shoving her.

Adjusting to rules in each foster home has been difficult for Greta. Before their removal, she and her sister faced no consequences for their misbehavior. Now, she is easily angered by foster parents' application of appropriate consequences for rule infringement. Although she will argue with foster parents about rules and consequences, Greta does not become aggressive toward them. Greta reported having suicidal thoughts following her removal and has considered cutting herself with a razor blade; she denies having suicidal or homicidal ideation while living in her parents' home. Two weeks ago, Greta wrapped the cord hanging from a window blind around her neck; she took it off when Sylvia entered the room; Sylvia seemingly did not notice Greta's apparent attempt at self-harm. At school last week, while her class was on the playground, Greta wrapped one of the chains from a swing set around her neck. A student persuaded her to stop, but the student kept what she had seen to herself.

Greta's academic record is excellent (all A's) and she is well-behaved at school, getting along well with her teachers and fellow students. She has never been given detention or suspension. She does not engage in alcohol or drug use. However, Greta has had difficulty adjusting to a strict dress code enforced at her new school, and she recently ended her participation in the school band.

Sylvia has alternate manic and depressive mood episodes. During depressive episodes Sylvia withdraws socially, has no appetite for food, cannot concentrate, and struggles to get even four hours' sleep at night. Always feeling tired, she loses interest in activities and pays little attention to her surroundings. Furthermore, paranoiac feelings make her uncomfortable around people, who she thinks are watching her. She is easily irritated and often snaps verbally at others. During manic mood episodes,

Sylvia is extremely sociable and energetic, so energetic that she sleeps no more than two hours nightly. Her appetite returns and she may gain a little weight. In her elevated mood, Sylvia spends a great deal of time talking with friends. Despite these episodes, Sylvia receives A and B grades and gets along with the teachers and students in school.

Prior to entering foster care, Sylvia revealed that she had performed oral sex acts for her father. Sylvia argued daily with her mother. Their mutual lack of affection and respect was often expressed in violence. The mother once held Sylvia against a wall and choked her, cutting off her breathing. The mother regularly threw objects at Sylvia and twisted Sylvia's arm up painfully behind her back. When the sisters used to have supervised visitation with their parents, Sylvia would become uncomfortable in her father's presence. She sometimes experiences flashbacks of the sexual abuse, feeling disgusted, angry, and upset. Sylvia is afraid to be by herself in a room, and she persistently fears that someone has come into her room at night. Sylvia sometimes cries as she thinks about the physical abuse.

3.1.3 Quenton

Susan (age 37) and Jason (age 38) are the parents of Quenton (age 13) and Alexis (age 11).

Quenton suffers from anxiety, which makes his hands tremble and causes him to avoid eye contact. He has low self-esteem and manages stress poorly, although he endures a lot of it. He is teased in a degrading way at school, which creates some of his stress; he loses a good deal of sleep over this, and sleep deprivation is accompanied by poor appetite. Those schoolmates with whom Quenton does not get along are primarily a group of "popular" students. They criticize his appearance, calling him "ugly." They repeatedly approach him and push him unexpectedly from behind; he yells obscenities at them in return. The bullying is ongoing, although Quenton has reportedly informed school staff about it. Quenton does not discuss with his parents the teasing and bullying he experiences all school year long. He sometimes cries when he is alone, though. Last school year, he failed a math course.

Quenton complies with the rules of his household; he does his chores without objection. While he dislikes how closely Jason supervises him, he does not behave in an aggressive way and he does not have emotional outbursts. Quenton often feels lonely. He spends free time playing video games alone. He feels that other children are "better" than he is.

Quenton uses alcohol, cigarettes, and marijuana. He took up tobacco at age 10 and typically smokes two cigarettes each day to alleviate his stress. Susan reportedly provides him with cigarettes. Neighbors of the family provide him with the marijuana he uses weekly. He has declined to share how frequently he drinks to the point of intoxication. Quenton has never been subjected to child abuse or neglect at home; he does not have a record of juvenile delinquency.

While he denies having homicidal thoughts, Quenton has made several attempts at suicide. Six months ago, he cut his wrist with a steak knife after his father slapped and yelled at him because Alexis had reported Quenton's marijuana use to Jason. For about the past month, Quenton has felt unable to bear all the burdens. His feelings led him to cut his wrist again, in the middle of the night. He then sought help from a neighbor, who summoned police. This suicide attempt left Quenton hospitalized for a week. He has now returned home following his discharge from the hospital.

Susan was abandoned by her own mother at age two. Susan's Aunt Lucy cared for her after that, and Susan has had no subsequent contact with the biological mother. Susan graduated from high school and completed a 16-week training course for medical assistants. Her employment, however, has been limited to factory jobs and fast-food work. Susan has had frequent conflicts with co-workers everywhere she has worked. She apparently cannot hold any job for long.

Susan is a pack-a-day smoker and admits she uses marijuana with friends in their homes; her friends provide the marijuana. Jason worries about her marijuana use, mostly due to the money it costs. Jason has explained to her that their budget cannot accommodate her habit, but Susan appears unready to give up marijuana. As a young adult, Susan experienced some legal trouble, spending one day in jail after an incident of breaking and entering; she then received a year's probation.

Jason, raised by his biological mother and an extremely strict stepfather, does not know his biological father's whereabouts. Jason has reportedly never experienced physical or sexual abuse as a child. Both mother and stepfather did not use alcohol or drugs. Jason has four stepsisters.

Jason is a temporary worker in a metal factory. Twice each week he consumes a 40-ounce beer; he claims that he consumes no other alcohol or recreational drug. Beer does not make Jason violent, and he appears able, when necessary, to limit his drinking. For example, when working the metal factory's second shift, he reportedly consumes no alcohol before or after work. He has explained that a clear head is required to do his job safely. The weight of the equipment he uses and of the loads of materials involved in the manufacturing poses a constant danger. In his free time, Jason enjoys televised sports, his viewing accompanied by beer drinking.

Alexis can be moody and defiant. At times her defiance is difficult for her parents to handle. Alexis hates to be told "No." Alexis sometimes argues with Quenton over their chores and their use of the family's video gaming equipment. Still, she gets along with people at her school and is a member of the school soccer team. Alexis furthermore earns good grades (despite occasionally forgetting to submit homework by its due date).

3.2 Anxiety—Henry

3.2.1 Henry

Henry (age 8) and his mother sought help from a social worker when, for several months, the same nightmare troubled Henry repeatedly. In the nightmare, an alien or monster was eating Henry. He had become fearful and could not fall asleep at night, believing an alien or monster could come to his room as he slept and tear open his tummy. During this period, Henry complained often that he had a stomachache. His mother had begun feeling very concerned; she believed that by saying prayers, she and Henry could calm his fears so that he could sleep. Concerning other aspects of Henry's life, his mother reported that he was doing well generally and had no trouble at school.

Henry and his brother Scott (age 7) argued or fought frequently over toys. Henry tended to talk back to his parents when they intervened in the quarreling. At his most recent birthday party, which was held at the family's home, Henry had become very excited. He made a remark about his genitals, prompting his parents to correct him, instructing him not to speak of private parts at a party. During the party, Henry and Scott began to fight over a toy Henry had received as a birthday present; Henry pushed Scott down and touched Scott's genitals. His parents stopped Henry's inappropriate touching but said the brothers could tickle other places on each other's bodies.

An older brother in the family, Allen (age 11), had been adopted some years earlier. Prior to the adoption, Allen had been abused physically and sexually in his biological family. He did not undertake counseling to address that abuse. Allen often stayed in his own room to play video games. He showed both anxiety and depressive symptoms, disliking contacting peers, talking little, and seldom discussing his feelings. He did not have suicidal thoughts. In school, Allen earned B and C grades in his classes; the school had never expressed concern about his academic performance or his behavior. At one point during the period Henry had the repeated nightmare, his parents filed a report when Henry complained to them vaguely that a person had initiated sexual contact with him. The report was not substantiated, due to Henry's persistent use of the terms *alien* and *monster*. Later, Allen admitted he might have done something with Henry that he was not certain constituted abuse. Allen denied ongoing sexual abuse or sexualized activities of any kind in the family's home. Each boy had his own room, and when the children were together, the parents were typically quite watchful.

3.3 ADHD—Polo

3.3.1 Polo Family

Ms. Polo and Tony (age 9) lived together. Teacher reported to CPS when she found finger marks on Tony's face. CPS investigated and substantiated that Ms. Polo had slapped Tony's face out of anger. Tony was then placed in father's care temporarily. CPS referred the family to a family preservation program for reunification.

Tony's parents were divorced three years ago because they could not get along. Tony had been in his mother's custody and maintained frequent contact with his father. Mother and Tony were living in a trailer park. Father was living with his girlfriend and her children several miles away.

Ms. Polo was injured in a car accident one year ago and had several surgeries on her leg. She was often in pain and required medication to ease the pain. She complained about Tony's difficult behavior. Tony was diagnosed with attention deficit hyperactivity disorder (ADHD), but his medication did not always calm him down. Tony often ran in the house and jumped on the sofa. He had difficulty following her instruction. He often had temper tantrums and argued with his mother about the morning routine (e.g., waking up, brushing teeth, and choosing clothes). Mother's limited mobility often meant she could not stop him from doing things. Tony often disagreed with his mother and talked back to her. When his mother physically halted his hyperactive behavior, Tony would become angry and kick her injured leg. Mother then became angry and slapped him with her open hand. Mother admitted that she was very frustrated but she never used anything else other than her open hand to punish Tony's out-of-control behavior.

Tony could not concentrate at school and schoolwork was very difficult for him. Other students teased him and that made him angry. He sometimes fought with other students. He did not like his teacher because he felt that he was not her favorite.

Reportedly, he listened to his father's instruction because his father seemed more serious. He enjoyed spending time with his father and father's girlfriend.

Ms. Polo has been receiving Temporary Assistance for Needy Families (TANF) benefits and food stamps while she and Tony were living together.

3.4 Bipolar Disorder—Martha

3.4.1 Martha

Martha (age 25) and her one-year-old boy were investigated by CPS. There was little food found in the house. There was no heat or water in the apartment because Martha did not pay her bills for several months. Her landlord was threatening to evict her because she was several months behind on her rent. CPS agreed that Martha and her son could remain together if she resolved her problem as soon as possible. Martha also agreed to work with family preservation program.

Martha was working full-time in a small company. Her weekly salary was enough for her to afford her necessities. Martha was diagnosed with bipolar disorder. She had cycles of depression and elevated moods. She also had spending sprees after receiving her weekly paycheck. She would buy things before she paid her bills. For instance, she once bought two toilets after she cashed her paycheck. She often felt lonely and unhappy, and she liked to have her friends spend time at her apartment. Her friends would eat her food and use her phone for long-distance calling. Consequently, she had little food left in the apartment and she could not afford the phone services. She was not compliant with her medication and did not regularly attend psychotherapy.

Martha had little support from relatives. Although her mother was very frustrated with Martha's persistent problem and refused to help her financially, Martha left her son in her mother's care while she went to work. Martha refused to seek or receive help from her son's father. They were not married and had broken up because he had an affair.

3.5 PTSD—Marcus and Carrie

3.5.1 Marcus and Carrie

Marcus (age 29) and Carrie (age 28), were married for 10 years, living with their children—Annie (age 10) and Shane (age 7).

Marcus believed in strict disciplinary parenting methods, the same way that he grew up. Marcus became angry with any disobedience from Annie or Shane. Marcus would yell at them, but he would not physically punish them. On the other hand, Carrie believed that reasoning and affection were *the* parenting method. While Carrie spent most time in housekeeping and spent little time with the children, Marcus enjoyed playing with them.

Marcus and Carrie had a dysfunctional marital relationship and alleged domestic violence. They had separated several times due to Marcus's extramarital affairs.

Marcus felt bored by the marriage, and he showed no regret of his infidelity. The most recent separation happened six months ago. Carrie suspected and confronted Marcus's relationship with a woman for months. When she could not tolerate any more, she kicked Marcus out of the house. After Marcus took a vacation with his mistress, Carrie forgave him, and he moved back in two months ago. The marital relationship had been filled with affection, intimacy, and respect for one month. Two weeks ago, however, Marcus came home late and intoxicated. He and Carrie argued, and Marcus choked Carrie and pushed her against the wall. Witnessing this violent episode, Shane began screaming on the floor while Annie yelled and cursed at Marcus. Marcus was so angry that he threw Annie into the sofa. Then Marcus ran out of the house and did not come home that night. Carrie did not call the police; both Carrie and Annie suffered no bruises.

Marcus was a heavy drinker but believed that he had no drinking problem. Heavy drinking was not uncommon among his parents and relatives. He drank a dozen 16-oz cans of beer each day. He drank with his co-workers at a bar after work each day. He claimed that drinking did not affect his performance at the construction site. Carrie confirmed that his breath had strong odor of alcohol when he came home after work. Shane reported that Marcus often walked and talked funny at home after work; Marcus also bumped into furniture in the house. Marcus was intoxicated very often but he denied any blackouts. Annie reported that Marcus lay on the floor and had no response for hours once or twice per week. Marcus did not seek or attend any substance abuse treatment program.

Carrie was diagnosed with depression for several years but her participation in counseling and psychiatric treatment had been sporadic. She suffered crying spells and had difficulty of fall asleep at night; consequently, she often felt fatigued. She took prescribed medication to help her to sleep. She occasionally felt anxious and irritated. She also reportedly "saw" several huge spiders crawling on her arms last week. Carrie had been a housewife since she was married. While Carrie and Marcus were separated six months ago, Carrie became the sole provider for her children. She worked part-time for a car dealership, and the family relied on TANF and food stamps. Carrie's parents had been financially and emotionally supportive. After Marcus and Carrie reunited, Carrie kept the part-time job. Since the last violent episode, Carrie considered divorce but worried about potential financial difficulties. Marcus considered divorce a sign of his personal failure.

Annie had posttraumatic stress disorder (PTSD) symptoms. She experienced flashbacks of her parents' violent episodes. She had nightmares and wet her bed at night. She was easily agitated and argued with her parents. She screamed at Marcus if he confronted her. Annie and Shane fought over toys and Annie would kick and punch him. Annie did not get along with her classmates and she punched them as well. Her grades were dropping and she could not pay attention in class. Interestingly, Annie reportedly had no behavior or performance problem at home or school while her parents were separated. Annie wished that her parents were divorced but also worried about the financial condition.

Shane was withdrawn but explosive at times. He was quiet and did not share his feelings. He did not like Annie because she was aggressive toward him. Shane's performance in school was average. He had only a few friends. Shane did not like the idea of his parents divorcing.

3.6 Personality Disorder—Sean and Sophia

3.6.1 *Sean and Sophia*

Sean (age 35) and Sophia (age 33) had been married for 11 years. They and their three children—Jordan (age 11), Mick (age 9), and Kelly (age 8)—lived in a farmhouse.

Sean drank 24 16-oz beers at home each day. He was intoxicated every other day. He had blackouts at least twice per month. He had been a supervisor of a machinery shop for five years. He earned good wages and owned the family's small house. He rigidly demanded Sophia and Jordan keep the house clean and proper. He screamed and cursed at them if they did not clean the house or if they broke something in the house. If they talked back to him, he held up his fist and threatened to hit them.

Sophia showed schizotypal personality disorder symptoms. Her mood was monotonic. She had difficulty making conversation and focusing on the topic of discussion. Her speech and thinking were confusing and vague. She believed that she had some supernatural power to influence others' minds. She had burned Sean's and the children's clothing several times in the woods behind the house because she believed that would control their behavior. She suspected that Sean and children were trying to get rid of her. She had no friends, and her relatives did not contact the family. Sean's relatives teased him about Sophia's odd behavior and made fun of her. She did not have any psychiatric evaluation or service in the past.

Jordan was ashamed of her parents' behavior. She had no close friends and never invited anyone to the home. She was fearful that someone would see the beer bottles or cans on the floor and her drunken father. She disliked her father's screaming and threats. She did not like to do chores because her father checked repeatedly. She disliked the uncles and aunts who made fun of her mother. Although she perceived that her mother was odd, Jordan did not believe that her mother was "crazy." However, Jordan did worry that she would become like her mother in the future. Furthermore, she did not trust her mother on "women's issues." She smoked cigarettes and she was angry that her parents searched her room.

Jordan was easily agitated and aggressive at school. Students complained that she picked fights, something she denied doing. She became very angry if other students provoked her. She punched them in the face and kicked them in the stomach. She had B's in the last school year, but she had C's for her classes this year. She wore black clothing, lipsticks, and nail polish. She had a dark vision of the world that she talked about death and sickness in the class. She was caught smoking in the school.

3.7 Intimate Partner Violence—Beth; Vivian

3.7.1 *Beth*

Beth (age 34) discussed her marital problems with a social worker. Her husband, Peter (age 40), was not interested in marital counseling. They had been married for five years and had two children. Reportedly, Peter had been overly protective as well as controlling, of Beth. Beth wanted to work again after the children began attending school. Peter, a religious man, believed that Beth should be a housewife and exclusively take care of the children. Due to this issue, Peter sometimes became verbally abusive to Beth. Recently, he began to shove Beth when she expressed her desire to work. Beth grew up in a religious family and some friends of their church agreed with Peter's viewpoint.

3.7.2 *Vivian*

Vivian (age 25) and Jacob (age 27) were married for six years; they have been separated for one month. Their biological children, Dustin (age 5) and Sarah (age 3), live with Vivian.

Vivian sought help from an agency because Dustin could not control his temper at home. He had become easily agitated, having temper tantrums on a daily basis. He had thrown objects at, punched, and bitten Sarah. He has not been complying with "time-out."

Dustin was very cooperative in the meeting with the social worker. He was calm and used good manners. Despite a stutter, he was expressive. He had difficulty falling asleep and had many nightmares. He was worried about the safety of his mother and sister. He observed that his father beat up his mother. Reportedly, his father threw objects at his mother and punched her in the stomach. At times when Dustin witnessed this violence, he would run to his room and cry.

Vivian revealed that Jacob had been physically abusive to her. The aggression allegedly began two years earlier. Before then, Jacob had been only verbally abusive. The initial physical violence (Jacob grabbing Vivian's arms and pushing her) occurred in the presence of both children. Eventually, he began throwing objects (mugs and pictures) at her and punching and kicking her, leaving bruises and cuts on her body. Jacob choked Vivian several times, too. Developing psychosomatic symptoms (vomiting and hyperventilation) prompted Vivian to take the children and move away. She suggested divorce to Jacob. He became very angry and called Vivian threatening to "cut" her face and kill her. Vivian was very frightened and cried alone. She is afraid to leave her home or go to work. Reportedly, Jacob has stood outside the apartment at times, drinking beer and screaming. He also has stood outside Vivian's workplace. Vivian feels helpless and does not know what to do. She does not want to tell her parents, who had discouraged her from marrying Jacob.

Vivian's biological parents have been married for over 50 years. Vivian had a happy childhood. She has no history of mental health problems or drug use. She graduated from high school and became a factory worker.

Jacob's biological father left him and his mother when he was five years old. Jacob reportedly has been physically abused by his stepfather. Jacob abuses marijuana and alcohol.

3.8 Parent–Teenager Conflict—Nelson

3.8.1 *Nelson*

Nelson (age 50) had diabetes for 10 years. He and his biological son, Tyler (age 16), lived together. They sought help from the family agency to resolve their relationship conflicts.

Nelson reported no history of abuse or neglect in his childhood. He was the youngest and the only one who completed high school. He then moved to the city and worked in a factory. His parents were living, but they lived barely above the poverty line. Nelson and Heather (age 45) were married and had three children—Faye (age 25), Tyler, and Terrell (age 12).

Nelson was diagnosed with diabetes about 10 years ago. His depressive and angry reaction to the illness spilled over into his marital relationship. Nelson and Heather eventually divorced about five years ago. After the divorce, Nelson had custody of Tyler, and Heather had custody of Terrell. Faye had moved out to the college.

Despite receiving medical attention, Nelson's diabetic conditions gradually deteriorated. He lost several toes because of the illness. He easily got tired and his vision was failing. He could not work and relied on Supplemental Security Income (SSI) for seven years. He once fell into a diabetic coma and could not wake up in the morning. Fortunately, Tyler rescued Nelson by giving him an injection. Nelson was very watchful for his diet. He was very frustrated because he had been waiting for a transplant for years. He recognized that he would soon die if there was no transplant for him.

Tyler was very angry with his father. Tyler perceived that Nelson was responsible for the break-up of the family. Tyler saw his father as impotent and useless. Tyler was tired of checking his father every morning. He complained that he was the only one doing the chores at home. He accused his father of collecting "junk" at home. Furthermore, he complained about his father's cooking. Tyler also complained that he could spend little time with his friends, because his father did not allow him to use the family car to visit them. Subsequently, he spent a lot of time and money on the internet for entertainment and communication with his friends. Tyler and Nelson often argued over money. Once Nelson allegedly held an axe and threatened to destroy Tyler's computer. In the same incident, Tyler screamed at Nelson and threatened to destroy his collections. Tyler showed little emotion about his father's medical conditions.

Tyler wished to live with Heather. However, visitation with Heather and Terrell had been tense and hostile. Tyler accused Heather of favoritism and Terrell of "spoiled" behavior. Tyler and Terrell argued and physically fought in each visitation. Therefore, Heather had refused visitation with Tyler for several months. This fueled Tyler's anger and he displaced it on to Nelson.

3.9 Sibling Rivalry—Patricia and Ron

3.9.1 Patricia and Ron

Jenny (age 30) is the single mother of Patricia (age 13) and Ron (age 10). She left school in eleventh grade when she became pregnant with Patricia. She lived for several years with Patricia's father. Reportedly their relationship ended because Jenny felt the man attempted to control her every act. Later, Jenny lived with the man who became Ron's father. Jenny did not get along with him when he was drinking. The final breakup occurred two years ago, and Jenny left with the children.

Jenny has never received child support from Patricia's or Ron's father. She has struggled to raise the two children by herself and to achieve financial independence through her work for a department store for many years. She sometimes finds it difficult to manage her household budget.

Jenny has a history of mental illness. At 14 years of age, two weeks of her memory disappeared. Jenny's parents did not seek a medical explanation of or care for this memory loss. In her adulthood, she had been attending psychotherapy to address bipolar disorder. A few years earlier, she had been hospitalized for auditory hallucinations.

At seven years old, Patricia was diagnosed with ADHD. Her symptoms reportedly were not alleviated by prescribed medications she tried. At home with her family, Patricia is argumentative and defiant. She behaves aggressively toward Ron, because she feels she is continually competing with him for Jenny's favor. Patricia regularly yells at Ron, sometimes pushing or kicking him. Ron has turned up with unexplained bruises and other marks of injury. Jenny is watchful when Patricia is interacting with Ron.

Patricia likes calling her friends, while Ron is an avid online gamer. The two will fight about use of both the phone line and the family's video console and games. In one incident, Ron sat atop of Patricia, nearly suffocating her accidentally because a pillow constricted her breathing. Patricia told Jenny what had happened, and Jenny lectured Ron.

Patricia failed a science class at school. She engaged in name-calling with fellow students and sometimes throwing objects at them or pushing them. Patricia has been suspended from school twice because she had hit a student.

Patricia has consumed alcohol, under pressure from the friends with whom she tries to fit in. Last month, she finished her first full can of beer. She recently has consumed up to three cans, while visiting a friend's home. Patricia drinks not just when she is socializing, but also when she is unhappy.

Ron is hyperactive and inattentive, often running and jumping indoors at home and little able to maintain eye contact or concentrate, both at home and in school. He shifts constantly from activity to activity, unless he is gaming online. He is easily frustrated and argumentative. He challenges Jenny over meals, TV, and bedtime, and he refuses to clean his room. He behaves aggressively toward pets.

Last year, Ron was diagnosed with ADHD. The medication prescribed for him reportedly improved his behavior. When Jenny decided his ADHD should be addressed via his diet, Ron stopped the medication. His ADHD symptoms have resumed.

Ron also suffers from anxiety, especially at night. Once each month he is unable to sleep at all for a 48-hour stretch, and when he can sleep, he is a habitual sleepwalker. Often at bedtime he is fully preoccupied with the thought of being chased by a monster, which is the theme of his favorite video game. Moreover, Ron has reported visual hallucinations, "seeing" unspecified small animals running inside the family's house, as well as words on the TV screen that Jenny or Patricia could or did not see. Ron once "saw" a body in a freezer inside a grocery store.

Ron's grades include several D's. In class, he frequently lays his head down on his desk and refuses to work on his assignments. When a teacher insists, Ron makes the least effort possible. Ron cannot get along with peers at school, who often mock his appearance and his beliefs. Ron is an atheist with no belief in a god. He also believes that lawless violence, revenge, and reversion to primitive living conditions are good countermeasures to the burgeoning human population. He has talked about various approaches to the commission of school massacres, and his teacher is deeply concerned about his dark, disturbing ideas. Ron reportedly uses no alcoholic or other substances.

3.10 Teenage Pregnancy—Sharon

3.10.1 Sharon

Sharon (age 13) sought advice from a social worker for her crisis. She and her boyfriend had just found out that she was pregnant. Her boyfriend did not want to be a father or to take care of the baby. She was a very good student and planned to attend college. The thought of becoming a mother frightened her and she had considered abortion. She had not discussed the pregnancy with her religious parents.

3.11 Chronic Illness—Elma; Fred

3.11.1 Elma

At age 10, Paula (age 29) was physically abused by her stepmother. Additionally, from age eight to 10, she was molested by one of her uncles. Subsequently, Paula spent five years in foster care. After she was adopted, her adoptive parents helped Paula find her biological mother, although no ongoing relationship resulted. At age 19, Paula moved out of her adoptive parents' home. She maintains a relationship with her adoptive parents, visiting them each month. She has worked as a cashier in a party supply store for a decade.

Paula and Dan had a brief, violent relationship. They had no children together. Reportedly, Dan used alcohol, cocaine, marijuana, and other drugs. Dan abused Paula by throwing her, hitting her, and punching her. After Dan choked her the first time, Paula called the police. Even after they had divorced, Dan continued to stalk Paula and threaten her life; she obtained a restraining order against him. Paula reportedly suffers flashbacks and nightmares related to Dan's violent behavior. She often bursts out cursing at sudden loud noises in the area or when neighbors start up loud music.

Paula met Codi (age 33) and married him eight years ago. The couple and their two children today reside in a two-bedroom apartment. Codi's brother Matt occasionally visits them, and Paula's adoptive mother sometimes babysits their children. The softspoken Codi works in a bakery as a baker. Reportedly, his childhood included no abuse or neglect. Codi left school in the eleventh grade. He found work at a horse stable, where he washed and groomed the animals for four years.

Codi and Paula's children are Lori (age 7) and Elma (age 6). The sisters wear clothes that are clean. Lori appears healthy as well as on target developmentally speaking. She is active and plays with Elma, and she also likes spending time reading at the public library located next door to her family's apartment. Lori generally likes school and earns A's and B's; Paula helps Lori with homework. Lori's favorite subject is art; she wants to become a doctor one day. Lori does chores like dishwashing and taking out the trash.

Born at 26 weeks gestational age, Elma has many health problems and indications of developmental delay. At birth her heart and lungs were not strong. The six-year-old has asthma and ongoing heart problems of a potentially congestive nature, both of which will require long-term if not life-long medical attention. The hearing in each of her ears is impaired. She has a painful clubfoot condition on one side, and she did not walk until the age of four. She is so energetic that she is awake most nights until midnight. She ignores parental instructions and whines about the consequences of failing to follow her instructions.

Elma engages in four to five temper tantrums weekly. She throws objects or bangs her head into walls. Her easily sparked irritation can lead her to curse at others, make obscene gestures at others, and express physical aggression toward others. Elma's curiosity appears to exceed her capacity to perceive danger. She has dragged chairs up to cupboards in order to climb up and handle various items. Despite having burned herself on a stove as well as on a clothes iron, Elma continues to handle and turn on electric appliances. She does not pick up after herself.

Codi and Paula are overwhelmed; their parenting skills concerning Elma's special needs are limited. In addition, they find it difficult to manage household expenses, which include many medical and pharmacy bills associated with Elma's disabilities. Elma's higher-than-average number of medical appointments creates work conflicts for Paula and Codi. The couple uses time-out in an effort to discipline Elma, but the child has learned to use the need to "potty" to defeat the strategy.

3.11.2 Fred

Linda (age 31) is a single mother of Fred (age 13). Linda grew up free from any experience of child abuse or neglect. Her parents have been divorced for 10 years. Linda contacts her father infrequently. In contrast, she sees her brother about once a month; he lives in another town, and he used to help her maintain and repair her car.

Linda graduated from high school and subsequently enrolled in nurses' training. She did not finish the training, because she got involved with Fred's biological father. They divorced three years ago. Then Linda and Fred lived with Chris (age 35). Chris used both alcohol and cocaine. He was abusive to Linda, once throwing a shovel at the back of her right hand and left a two-inch scar. Two months ago, Chris and his drunken friends terrified the family by breaking dishes, windows, and the glass in Linda's car. Linda reported the vandalization of her home to police. Because Linda and Chris had allowed the men into the home, charges against the men were not pursued. Soon after, Chris left Linda and moved to a different state.

Linda is employed as a teamster. She saved money enough to buy her current two-bedroom home. While Linda claims not to use illicit drugs, recent urinalysis returned results positive for both cocaine and marijuana.

Fred suffers from depressive mood and anxiety. Additionally, he has had a diagnosis of diabetes for three years, and his condition has been deteriorating. Having a chronic illness makes Fred angry. He dislikes the diet he must follow and the insulin shots he must take. When angry, he often argues with Linda, subsequently becoming moody or withdrawn. Fred often feels useless, worthless, or sad; he often misses his father. During the time Chris lived in his home, Fred was often afraid of him, fearing his violent behavior toward Linda and resenting the way Chris bossed him around. Fred does not discuss his feelings with Linda.

It takes Fred until midnight or later to get to sleep every night, and he fails to sleep through the night as often as three times a week. Almost daily, Fred thinks of hurting himself. Upset about his medical problem, he once used a table knife to scratch into his upper arm. He sometimes thinks of killing himself. Fred has auditory hallucinations during which a female voice tells him to cut himself.

At home, Fred whines about his chores and regularly refuses to do them. Once Fred charged at Linda as if in a physical attack, but at the last moment he stopped. He argues with Linda over his carbohydrate and sugar intake and his insulin shots. Linda strives to regulate Fred's diet in order to manage his diabetes. Trying to reduce her son's cravings for sweet foods, Linda provides him with a limited supply of soft drinks; Fred is also allowed popcorn and fruit juice. He behaves kindly toward family pets.

Fred is well-behaved at school, earning B's and C's and getting along with others. Teachers have never complained about him, and he has no record of skipping a class, skipping school, being given detention, or being suspended. Fred reportedly has never tried any illicit substance, and he has never run away from home or played with fire.

3.12 School Violence—Owen; Rick

3.12.1 Owen

Viola (age 33) grew up a witness to violence between her biological mother and father. They reside in another town and she has not seen them for several months. She sees her two sisters comparatively often, although they reside in another state. Viola left school in the eleventh grade, after her son Owen was conceived. She wanted to finish her high school education. She actually enrolled in a program to do so, but she became pregnant a second time and dropped out. The child was stillborn.

Later, Viola married the children's father, Mario. They divorced after three years of marriage because Viola engaged in extramarital relationships. She and her second husband, Richard, have passed their third wedding anniversary. They and Owen (age 15) live in a two-bedroom apartment that is clean and tidy and comfortably furnished. Formerly working as a server in a series of restaurants, Viola now works full-time as a driver for a factory. She has admitted to using marijuana four times recently with her friends. In addition, Viola typically goes through one dozen 12-ounce beers every two days.

Richard (age 40) was reportedly abused during his childhood. His father passed away when Richard was only four; these days, his mother is dependent on alcohol. He has a sister and a brother who live in a different state. The three grew up in a neighborhood controlled by youth gangs. To survive, Richard joined one, and at 16 his role in it led to six months' placement in a residential facility for juveniles. When he was released, Richard's mother would not allow him back into her home, citing his involvement with the gang. He continued to associate with the gang's members, participating in juvenile delinquency and ending up jailed several times.

Later, Richard moved away from the neighborhood and reportedly gave up all interaction with the gang. He now works full-time-plus as a mechanic, his employer purportedly impressed by Richard's reliability in the face of long daily shifts.

Richard took up cocaine use while he belonged to the gang. Meeting Viola motivated him to give up cocaine, although he does still consume marijuana with a marijuana-using client to whose home Richard occasionally delivers a repaired car. Richard enjoys hunting and has a shotgun.

Owen has conflict with Richard. Owen considers going to live with Mario. Owen disappoints that Mario sees him so infrequently. Owen displaces this disappointment—as well as frustration and anger—from Mario onto Richard. He openly disrespects Richard and believes Richard has no right to engage in parenting him. Usually, an argument between Owen and Richard turns into a physical fight. At the same time, Owen likes to accompany Richard on hunting trips. Owen gets into arguments with his mother and refuses to do his chores. He throws objects or punches the wall when he is angry.

When among his peers, Owen exercises poor judgment. A couple weeks ago, he and two fellow students used Richard's shotgun without permission and killed a stray dog behind Owen's apartment. Owen secretly knew the location of the gun cabinet key. He has shown no remorse at all over the incident.

Owen's grades in school have declined from C's to D's. Toward school authorities, Owen is oppositional and defiant. He dislikes his teachers and argues with them. He is frequently insubordinate, known to walk out of a classroom when riled. He does not get along with other students and has a history of school-based violent behavior. He used a rock to hit a student in the head, necessitating stitches and hospitalization. This resulted in a two-week suspension from school. Another "in-school" suspension, lasting one week, resulted from Owen physically fighting with a student in the hall. More recently, several students have reported that Owen claimed to have a plan to shoot students in his school on April 20. Owen denies ever making such remarks.

Owen smokes three or four cigarettes a day. He has gotten drunk two times in the past couple of months. He states that alcohol use does not have any negative outcomes.

3.12.2 Rick

Rick (age 11) is the only child of Rita (age 30). Rita married Jesse when she was 18 years old. Jesse is Rick's father. Over the years, Rita and Jesse have at times demeaned each other in front of Rick; they have told him contradictory tales about each other, which has confused and annoyed him.

During Jesse and Rita's marriage, Jesse abused drugs and had an affair with another man. Rita divorced him and then went through several unstable relationships. One ex-boyfriend was violent and once grabbed Rick and slammed him into a wall. Now, Rita is engaged with Luke. Their relationship is strong and they have lived together for two years.

Rita was born with spina bifida and curvature of the spine. She had back surgery when she was born, again at age two, and again at age 15. She has little feeling on the right side of her body and in her left foot as well. Walking is difficult for her. She also has trouble supervising and managing Rick's behavior. Rita works in a retail store. She is a frequent alcohol user.

Luke (age 42) has been married twice. The first marriage ended after 10 years when his first wife had an affair. One daughter was born to their marriage, and Luke has always maintained a relationship with her, paying child support through her 18th birthday and visiting her regularly. Following a divorce from his second wife, Luke was given custody of their son, Brian (age 10). Luke neither smokes, drinks alcohol, nor uses any illicit drug. He has worked for many years at one factory. Reportedly, he has no criminal record nor any history of involvement of any kind in child abuse or neglect. To Luke's mind, Rick and Brian's priorities should be obeying the rules and completing their educations.

Rick shows symptoms of psychomotor retardation. He gets irritated or angry quite easily; he sometimes punches himself in the head. Rick often feels sad, but he does not often talk about his feelings. Although his appetite is poor, he does sleep well and is not troubled by nightmares. He enjoys playing football.

Rick dislikes living with Rita, in part because she ignores him. He feels sad when she ignores him, and hour-long crying spells in his bedroom are not unusual for Rick. His mood is becoming increasingly unstable. He gets markedly angry with Rita daily, screaming at her and remarking hatefully, "I don't like you" and "I hate you." Rita tends to yell back and curse at Rick. Last month, his anger began to intensify noticeably. He spent last week visiting his maternal grandparents and balked at returning home when it was time. Rick dislikes Luke and Brian. He perceives Luke as a person attempting to replace Jesse.

While Rick reportedly does not have suicidal ideation, he does have homicidal ideation targeting Rita. In Rick's room Rita has found two pictures he drew that demonstrate his homicidal ideation. One shows a huge boulder falling down on top of Rita's head. The other shows an unidentifiable person who just shot Rita in the head with a gun. Rick has refused to say who the shooter in his picture is. He was very angry when drawing the two pictures. While Rick showed no remorse or guilt about his ideation or about making the drawings, he became upset upon learning that Rita has discovered the two drawings. Rick's maternal grandfather reportedly owns a gun.

Rick fights with Brian over clothing and other matters. Brian once went into Rick's room when Rick was out and put on some of Rick's clothes. Rick became very upset about over this intrusion by Brian. The boys' conflicts sometimes turn physical. Rick has punched Brian in the stomach hard enough to make Brian vomit blood. In another frightening incident, Brian threatened Rick with a hammer. Although Luke separated the boys, Brian left a two-inch gash and bruising on Rick's right arm. Neither Brian nor Rick exhibited any remorse over these incidents; neither views their physical altercations as a particular problem. The dangerous fight with the hammer was not reported to any authority, and Rita and Luke did not seek professional help for Brian and Rick to address the violent behavior.

Rick has a history of school truancy, including at his new school. When he does attend, he behaves aggressively. The school he was enrolled at last school year expelled Rick. The expulsion was the consequence of Rick's assault on a female student. He injured the student badly enough that she was hospitalized.

Brian has an even temper and stable mood. He eats and sleeps well. He largely complies with rules and follows instructions at home. He earns grades of A and B in his classes at school, and he gets along with fellow students well. He has no history of being given detention or suspended from school. He has reportedly never experimented with alcohol or other drugs. Brian does not like Rick. Brian likes to play chess.

4 Case Examples in Other Services

4.1 Elderly—Kathleen; Yu

4.1.1 Kathleen

Kathleen (age 75) had retired from her career as a school teacher and had been living by herself in the five years since her husband had passed away from cancer. Kathleen took a fall on a sidewalk about a week ago, breaking her left leg and left arm. She was hospitalized for her injuries. When she was discharged from the medical center two days ago, she returned to her home, where she continued using a wheelchair. As a result of her hospitalization, a social worker visited Kathleen at home. The social worker observed bruises on Kathleen's forearms and asked about them. Kathleen's response was silence and welling tears. Kathleen revealed that her son who had come to her home to provide her with help as she recovered had become so frustrated, he had pinched her arms and other places on her person. Kathleen also revealed that she had abused this son when he was a child. The son had stopped coming to Kathleen's home following the pinching incident. Kathleen has difficulty moving herself through her home in the wheelchair. Before breaking her leg and arm, Kathleen had regularly gone out to church services and stayed active in other church activities. She had enjoyed gardening in her yard and strolling around the neighborhood.

4.1.2 Yu

Mr. Yu (age 67) immigrated to this country four years ago. Initially, his son (age 35) and daughter-in-law (age 32) supported him after he immigrated. Mr. Yu had supported his son's graduate study in United States and his son is a civil engineer. His daughter-in-law is an American-born woman and is a sales manager for a department store. After a year, however, a serious conflict developed among the three, and Mr. Yu moved away. He also lost the financial support of his son and daughter-in-law. He has no other relatives in this country. Mr. Yu found work at a restaurant, but this year his employer "retired" him. He has no savings, and he is not eligible for Social Security. Presently he lives with some former co-workers from the restaurant, but he cannot afford his share of rent. In fact, the co-workers sometimes give Mr. Yu cash for needs other than rent. Still, he has too little money for adequate food and medicine. He has begun resorting to meals of his roommates' leftovers and even cat food. When sick, he turns to herbal medicine, remedies in which he has longed believed; he patronizes an herbal healer in his ethnic neighborhood.

DOI: 10.4324/9781003316688-4

The loss of his job due to his age and declining agility makes Mr. Yu feel frustrated and even angry. His search for another job has led nowhere; no one seems willing to hire him. He wishes that he could work as an English interpreter, as he was an English interpreter for the government of his home country. Talking about his son and their poor relationship makes him feel ashamed.

In the past month, Mr. Yu has developed some alarming symptoms. On two occasions he became lost in his own neighborhood. He has had to start writing notes to himself to ensure he takes care of necessary errands. He has begun spending significant amounts of time piling up newspapers in one place in the apartment, only to transport the newspapers to another spot. He has difficulty remembering his son's and roommates' names, and he has trouble doing simple calculations. He sometimes forgets how to shave.

This afternoon, Mr. Yu woke up in a hospital with a broken ankle placed in a cast. The medical staff told him he apparently was wandering in the streets when he suffered a fall, leading to the ankle injury as well as bruises on his face and arms. He is in pain, and he is frightened about the incident because he cannot remember any of it. The doctor will discharge Mr. Yu tomorrow.

4.2 Sexual Orientation and Transgender—Todd; Zack

4.2.1 Todd

Todd (age 15) and his parents came to seek therapy for Todd. Todd told his religious parents that he wanted to become a woman. He has been exploring surgical operations for such change. His parents were shocked and angry. They were angry because they were "good parents" and they raised him properly. The parents were ashamed and did not share Todd's revelation with anyone. They believed that Todd had to change his "sinful" desire. They threatened to disown Todd if he did not cooperate with the therapist.

Todd received A's and B's from his classes. He got along with other students at school. He never tried any substance.

4.2.2 Zack

Zack (age 16) recently came to school with clearly evident bruising on his face. School employees reported Zack's injury to Child Protective Services. The agency investigated and referred Zack's family to ABC Family Services agency. Zack's family includes his father Earl (age 45) and his stepmother. Zack's biological mother lives with her husband in a different state.

The bruising on Zack's face occurred when he and Earl fought after an unexpected confrontation. Arriving home early from work, Earl found Zack and a 15-year-old neighbor boy in Zack's bedroom having sex. The neighbor left Earl and Zack's apartment immediately; Earl forbad Zack to see the neighbor again. Earl and Zack at first fought verbally, yelling at each other. Zack soon confronted his father with the revelation that he is gay. This led Earl to call his son names, curse at him, and hit Zack's face with his hands. Earl insisted Zack seek therapy to change his sexual orientation, threatening to kick Zack out of his home if his sexual orientation did not change.

From that day on, Zack has been argumentative and defiant, engaging in "back-talk" and "mouthiness," especially with Earl. At least every couple of days, Zack and his father have a substantial argument. Still, when Earl insists on it, Zack will complete his customary chores, such as cleaning his room, doing dishes, taking out trash, and sweeping. Zack has started drinking beer when he feels unhappy, something Earl tolerates without issue.

Zack has behavior and academic problems at school. He does not get along with some of his fellow students and has been suspended more than once for hitting other students. Zack always earns A grades in music and in art; on the other hand, he fails his science and writing assignments. Zack has no record of juvenile delinquency.

Earl has a high school education and has worked for many employers. He has been fired from several mechanic jobs due to incompetence. Earl currently is an auto maintenance crewman in a repair shop.

Earl's right hand shakes, and it appears a similar problem is developing with his left leg. He has these difficulties as the result of a stroke two years ago. Since he lacked health insurance at the time, he did not obtain medical attention for the possible stroke.

5 Working Alliances

5.1 Building Working Alliances with Outpatient Clients

A *working alliance* or *therapeutic alliance* is a collaborative, goal-oriented, purposeful working relationship or partnership between social worker and client; it is chiefly characterized by reciprocal respect and empathy (Bordin, 1979; Castonguay, Constantino, & Holtforth, 2006; Crits-Christoph, Gibbons, & Hearon, 2006; Duncan, Miller, & Sparks, 2004; Graybeal, 2007; Horvath, 2001, 2006; Horvath et al., 2011). Working alliances are built on mutual acceptance of negative emotions, on judicious criticism, and on shared decision-making (Horvath, 2001, 2006). A social worker and client in a working alliance nurture their mutual respect, trust, understanding, and commitment and bring these to the development of treatment goals and activities (Bordin, 1983, 1994). In addition, the social worker in a working alliance supports the client's efforts to overcome maladaptive beliefs and behaviors (Ribeiro, Ribeiro, Goncalves, Horvath, & Stiles, 2013). This support is essential, even though the client shares responsibility for seeing that treatment goals are met (Luborsky, 1976). It is through the social worker's support and encouragement that the client feels secure and confident enough to change personal behavior.

A strong working alliance between the social worker and client may foster desirable changes in the perceptions and behavior of the client (Bordin, 1983). Successful alliances may alleviate interpersonal and adjustment difficulties clients are experiencing (Cheng & Lo, 2018; Cheng, Lo, & Womack, 2019; Dinger, Zilcha-Mano, McCarthy, Barrett, & Barber, 2013; Lilliengren, Falkenstrom, Sandell, Mothander, & Werbart, 2015; McEvoy, Burgess, & Nathan, 2013, 2014); they may contribute to the number and accuracy of clients' insights (Cheng & Lo, 2018). Therapeutic alliances promote depressive clients' reaching out to relatives, friends, and social groups (Cheng & Lo, 2018). Importantly, strong working alliances are associated with desirable outcomes across numerous psychotherapy models, mental disorders, and substance-use disorders (Barber et al., 2001; Castonguay et al., 2006; Crits-Christoph et al., 2006; Duncan et al., 2004; Graybeal, 2007; Horvath, 2005; Jung, Wiesjahn, & Lincoln, 2014; Meier, Donmall, McElduff, Barrowclough, & Heller, 2006; Meyer et al., 2002; Orlinsky, Ronnestad, & Willutzki, 2004; Piper et al., 1999; Zuroff & Blatt, 2006; Zuroff et al., 2000).

For social workers who are case managers, the desired working alliance with clients is, again, collaborative and based in reciprocal trust and the two parties' sense of self-worth and of rapport (Brun & Rapp, 2001; Buck & Alexander, 2006; Grube & Mendenhall, 2016; Redko, Rapp, Elms, Snyder, & Carlson, 2007; Simpson et al.,

DOI: 10.4324/9781003316688-5

2015; Wodarski, 2000). Moreover, clients' perception of alliance correlated with that of case managers, regardless of problem severity and case manager work experience (Cheng & Lo, 2022). Social workers providing case management function as advocates for and coordinators of services clients need to address their own and their families' problems (National Association of Social Workers, 2013). These social workers help clients execute service plans or case plans by supplying not just crucial information, but emotional support as well; they put clients in touch with service agencies, periodically check in with agency service providers, and mobilize social support for clients who may see the road ahead as long, daunting, even lonely (Grube & Mendenhall, 2016; Nath, Alexander, & Solomon, 2012; Ryan, Ford, Beadsmoore, & Muijen, 1999; Simpson et al., 2015; Vourlekis & Ell, 2007; Zweben et al., 2015). In the realm of community-based social services, strong case manager–client working alliances fostered improvement of problems clients faced (Cheng et al., 2019).

5.2 Building Working Alliance in Child Welfare Cases

In child welfare settings, especially, building strong working alliances is crucial to safety, first, and then to the achievement of the desired outcomes. But it can be tough to build such alliances. Adults involved in child maltreatment cases not uncommonly deny the existence of problems and refuse appropriate services available to them. Research has established that, across ethnic groups, such refusal often results in families' failure to obtain needed child welfare services (Cheng & Lo, 2012). As Figure 5.1 illustrates, social workers and therapists often intervene during a specific process (e.g., foster care placement, relative placement, and family preservation) in the child welfare system. Unsurprisingly, parents involved in the child welfare system may then perceive the social workers as monitors or interlopers, not helpers. Parents in the system can feel that their freedoms are threatened or gone; the response can be hostility toward the social worker and denial of problems' existence (Mirick, 2012, 2014). Parents may accuse the child welfare system of one-sided, fanatical fault-finding and of absolute eagerness to remove children from home. A parent in this frame of mind makes building therapeutic alliance challenging at best.

Collaborative engagement and working alliance of professionals in the child welfare system with parents they assist promote these parents' receipt of needed services (Cheng & Lo, 2021b), promote progress by the parents (Cheng & Lo, 2016b), and promote children's health (Cheng & Lo, 2016a). Additionally, substantiated re-reporting of child maltreatment is less likely when social workers/therapists have successfully established working alliances with parents (Cheng & Lo, 2015). What's more, among formerly neglected children placed with foster families long-term, the presence of working alliances is associated with better odds of reunification with birth parents (Cheng, 2010). This benefit attaching to social worker–client working alliances reflects the fact that these alliances position child welfare workers to accurately identify parents' needs and create case plans addressing them. Research also indicates that parents whose case plans specify the services their child welfare workers perceived them to need are more likely than other parents to get needed services (Cheng & Lo, 2020a, 2020b, 2021a, 2021b).

To date, published findings from social work research generally make obvious the importance of therapeutic or working alliances as a tool in interventions that seek a range of desirable outcomes for clients. Working with a client to

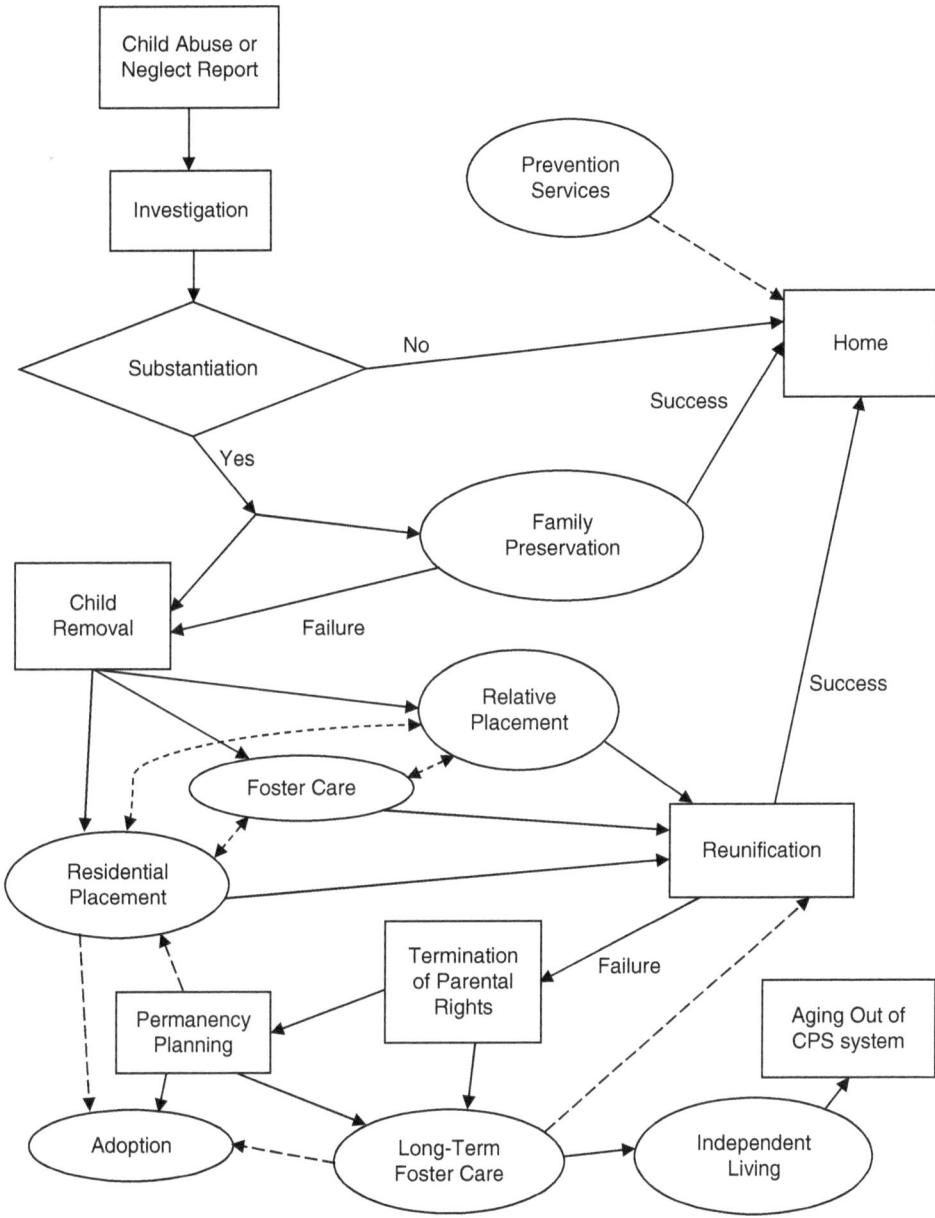

Figure 5.1 Child Protective Services: Process and Interventions.

develop—together—that client's case plan or intervention plan is one of the best opportunities a social worker employed in outpatient or child welfare settings will have to establish working alliance. Developing case plans and intervention plans are discussed in Chapter 6.

References

Barber, J. P., Luborsky, L., Gallop, R., Crits-Christoph, P., Frank, A., Weiss, R. D., ... Siqueland, L. (2001). Therapeutic alliance as a predictor of outcome and retention in the National Institute on Drug Abuse Collaborative Cocaine Treatment Study. *Journal of Consulting and Clinical Psychology*, 69(1), 119–124. doi:10.1037/0022-006x.69.1.119

Bordin, E. S. (1979). The genrealization of the psychoanalytic concept of the working alliance. *Psychotherapy: Theory, Research and Practice*, 16(3), 252–260.

Bordin, E. S. (1983). A working alliance based model of supervision. *Counseling Psychologist*, 11(1), 35–42. doi:10.1177/0011000083111007

Bordin, E. S. (1994). Theory and research on the therapeutic working alliance: New directions. In A. O. Horvath & L. S. Greenberg (Eds.), *The Working Alliance: Theory, Research, and Practice*. New York, NY: John Wiley & Sons, 13–37.

Brun, C., & Rapp, R. C. (2001). Strengths-based case management: Individuals' perspectives on strengths and the case manager relationship. *Social Work*, 46(3), 278–288. Retrieved from <Go to ISI>://WOS:000170087800008

Buck, P. W., & Alexander, L. B. (2006). Neglected voices: Consumers with serious mental illness speak about intensive case management. *Administration and Policy in Mental Health*, 33(4), 470–481. doi:10.1007/s10488-005-0021-3

Castonguay, L. G., Constantino, M. J., & Holtforth, M. G. (2006). The working alliance: Where are we and where should we go? *Psychotherapy*, 43(3), 271–279. doi:10.1037/0033-3204.43.3.271

Cheng, T. C. (2010). Factors associated with reunification: A longitudinal analysis of long-term foster care. *Children and Youth Services Review*, 32(10), 1311–1316. doi:10.1016/j.childyouth.2010.04.023

Cheng, T. C., & Lo, C. C. (2012). Racial disparities in access to needed child welfare services and worker-client engagement. *Children and Youth Services Review*, 34(9), 1624–1632. Retrieved from http://www.sciencedirect.com/science/article/pii/S019074091200179X

Cheng, T. C., & Lo, C. C. (2015). A longitudinal causal analysis of impact made by collaborative engagement and service receipt on likelihood of substantiated re-report. *Child Maltreatment*, 20(4), 258–267. doi:10.1177/1077559515597062

Cheng, T. C., & Lo, C. C. (2016a). Does collaborative engagement affect the health of young children in child welfare system? *Families in Society: The Journal of Contemporary Social Services*, 97(4), 305–311. doi:10.1606/1044-3894.2016.97.37

Cheng, T. C., & Lo, C. C. (2016b). Linking worker-parent working alliance to parent progress in child welfare: A longitudinal analysis. *Children and Youth Services Review*, 71, 10–16. doi:10.1016/j.childyouth.2016.10.028

Cheng, T. C., & Lo, C. C. (2018). A longitudinal analysis of factors associated with therapeutic alliances. *Community Mental Health Journal*, 54(6), 782–792. doi:10.1007/s10597-017-0229-1

Cheng, T. C., & Lo, C. C. (2020a). Mental health services receipt among caregivers in the child welfare system: A longitudinal analysis. *Children and Youth Services Review*, 113. doi:10.1016/j.childyouth.2020.104971

Cheng, T. C., & Lo, C. C. (2020b). Receipt of substance-use services by caregivers involved in the child-welfare system. *Children and Youth Services Review*, 112. doi:10.1016/j.childyouth.2020.104937

Cheng, T. C., & Lo, C. C. (2021a). When child welfare caseworkers intervene, do women surviving IPV obtain recommended services?. *Journal of Interpersonal Violence*, 36(21–22), NP11446–NP11463. doi:10.1177/0886260519888524

Cheng, T. C., & Lo, C. C. (2021b). With their children placed in kinship care, did parents get the services they needed? *Children and Youth Services Review*, 121. doi:10.1016/j.childyouth.2020.105850

Cheng, T. C., & Lo, C. C. (2022). Factors that contribute to strong working alliances between case managers and clients. *Journal of Social Work*, 1–14. doi:10.1177/14680173221083476

Cheng, T. C., Lo, C. C., & Womack, B. G. (2019). Working alliances promote desirable outcomes: A study of case management in the state of Alabama in the United States. *British Journal of Social Work*, 49, 147–162.

Crits-Christoph, P., Gibbons, M. B. C., & Hearon, B. (2006). Does the alliance cause good outcome? Recommendations for future research on the alliance. *Psychotherapy*, *43*(3), 280–285. doi:10.1037/0033-3204.43.3.280

Dinger, U., Zilcha-Mano, S., McCarthy, K. S., Barrett, M. S., & Barber, J. P. (2013). Interpersonal problems as predictors of alliance, symptomatic improvement and premature termination in treatment of depression. *Journal of Affective Disorders*, *151*(2), 800–803. doi:10.1016/j.jad.2013.07.003

Duncan, B. L., Miller, S. D., & Sparks, J. A. (2004). *The Heroic Client: A Revolutionary Way to Improve Effectiveness Through Client-Directed, Outcome-Informed Therapy*. San Francisco, CA: Jossey-Bass.

Graybeal, C. T. (2007). Evidence for the art of social work. *Families in Society-the Journal of Contemporary Social Services*, *88*(4), 513–523. doi:10.1606/1044-3894.3673

Grube, W., & Mendenhall, A. N. (2016). Adolescent mental health case management: Consumer perspectives. *Families in Society-the Journal of Contemporary Social Services*, *97*(2), 86–94. doi:10.1606/1044-3894.2016.97.13

Horvath, A. O. (2001). The alliance. *Psychotherapy*, *38*(4), 365–372. doi:10.1037/0033-3204.38.4.365

Horvath, A. O. (2005). The therapeutic relationship: Research and theory—An introduction to the Special Issue. *Psychotherapy Research*, *15*(1–2), 3–7. doi:10.1080/10503300512331339143

Horvath, A. O. (2006). The alliance in context: Accomplishments, challenges, and future directions. *Psychotherapy*, *43*(3), 258–263. doi:10.1037/0033-3204.43.3.258

Horvath, A. O., Del Re, A. C., Fluckiger, C., & Symonds, D. (2011). Alliance in individual psychotherapy. *Psychotherapy*, *48*(1), 9–16. doi:10.1037/a0022186

Jung, E., Wiesjahn, M., & Lincoln, T. M. (2014). Negative, not positive symptoms predict the early therapeutic alliance in cognitive behavioral therapy for psychosis. *Psychotherapy Research*, *24*(2), 171–183. Retrieved from <Go to ISI>://WOS:000330690800005

Lilliengren, P., Falkenstrom, F., Sandell, R., Mothander, P. R., & Werbart, A. (2015). Secure attachment to therapist, alliance, and outcome in psychoanalytic psychotherapy with young adults. *Journal of Counseling Psychology*, *62*(1), 1–13. doi:10.1037/cou0000044

Luborsky, L. (1976). Helping alliances in psychotherapy. In J. L. Cleghhorn (Ed.), *Successful Psychotherapy* (pp. 92–116). New York: Brunner/Mazel.

McEvoy, P. M., Burgess, M. M., & Nathan, P. (2013). The relationship between interpersonal problems, negative cognitions, and outcomes from cognitive behavioral group therapy for depression. *Journal of Affective Disorders*, *150*(2), 266–275. doi:10.1016/j.jad.2013.04.005

McEvoy, P. M., Burgess, M. M., & Nathan, P. (2014). The relationship between interpersonal problems, therapeutic alliance, and outcomes following group and individual cognitive behaviour therapy. *Journal of Affective Disorders*, *157*, 25–32. doi:10.1016/j.jad.2013.12.038

Meier, P. S., Donmall, M. C., McElduff, P., Barrowclough, C., & Heller, R. F. (2006). The role of the early therapeutic alliance in predicting drug treatment dropout. *Drug and Alcohol Dependence*, *83*(1), 57–64. doi:10.1016/j.drugalcdep.2005.10.010

Meyer, B., Pilkonis, P. A., Krupnick, J. L., Egan, M. K., Simmens, S. J., & Sotsky, S. M. (2002). Treatment expectancies, patient alliance, and outcome: Further analyses from the national institute of mental health treatment of depression collaborative research program. *Journal of Consulting and Clinical Psychology*, *70*(4), 1051–1055. doi:10.1037/0022-006x.70.4.1051

Mirick, R. G. (2012). Reactance and the child welfare client: Interpreting parents' resistance to services through the lens of reactance theory. *Families in Society-the Journal of Contemporary Social Services*, *93*(3), 165–172. doi:10.1606/1044-3894.4224

Mirick, R. G. (2014). The relationship between reactance and engagement in a child welfare sample. *Child & Family Social Work, 19*(3), 333–342. doi:10.1111/cfs.12022

Nath, S. B., Alexander, L. B., & Solomon, P. L. (2012). Case managers' perspectives on the therapeutic alliance: a qualitative study. *Social Psychiatry and Psychiatric Epidemiology, 47*(11), 1815–1826. doi:10.1007/s00127-012-0483-z

National Association of Social Workers. (2013). *NASW Standards of Social Work Case Management*. Retrieved from Washington, DC: National Association of Social Workers.

Orlinsky, D. E., Ronnestad, M. H., & Willutzki, U. (2004). Fifty years of psychotherapy process-outcome research: Continuity and change. In M. J. Lambert (Ed.), *Bergin and Garfield's Handbook of Psychotherapy and Behavior Change* (5th edition ed.). New York, NY: Johnson Wiley & Sons, 307–389.

Piper, W. E., Ogrodniczuk, J. S., Joyce, A. S., McCallum, M., Rosie, J. S., O'Kelly, J. G., & Steinberg, P. I. (1999). Prediction of dropping out in time-limited, interpretive: Individual psychotherapy. *Psychotherapy, 36*(2), 114–122. doi:10.1037/h0087787

Redko, C., Rapp, R. C., Elms, C., Snyder, M., & Carlson, R. G. (2007). Understanding the working alliance between persons with substance abuse problems and strengths-based case managers. *Journal of Psychoactive Drugs, 39*(3), 241–250. Retrieved from <Go to ISI>://WOS:000251217500005

Ribeiro, E., Ribeiro, A. P., Goncalves, M. M., Horvath, A. O., & Stiles, W. B. (2013). How collaboration in therapy becomes therapeutic: The therapeutic collaboration coding system. *Psychology and Psychotherapy-Theory Research and Practice, 86*(3), 294–314. doi: 10.1111/j.2044-8341.2012.02066.x

Ryan, P., Ford, R., Beadsmoore, A., & Muijen, M. (1999). The enduring relevance of case management. *British Journal of Social Work, 29*(1), 97–125. doi: http://www.jstor.org/stable/23714935

Simpson, A., Hannigan, B., Coffey, M., Jones, A., Barlow, S., Cohen, R., … Haddad, M. (2015). Study protocol: Cross-national comparative case study of recovery-focused mental health care planning and coordination (COCAPP). *Bmc Psychiatry, 15.* doi:10.1186/s12888-015-0538-2

Vourlekis, B., & Ell, K. (2007). Best practice case management for improved medical adherence. *Social Work in Health Care, 44*(3), 161–177. doi:10.1300/J010v44n03_03

Wodarski, J. S. (2000). The role for social workers in the managed health care system: A model for empirically based psycho-social interventions. *Crisis Intervention and Time-Limited Treatment, 6*(2), 109–139. Retrieved from <Go to ISI>://WOS:000165432400003

Zuroff, D. C., & Blatt, S. J. (2006). The therapeutic relationship in the brief treatment of depression: Contributions to clinical improvement and enhanced adaptive capacities. *Journal of Consulting and Clinical Psychology, 74*(1), 130–140. doi:10.1037/0022-006x.74.1.130

Zuroff, D. C., Blatt, S. J., Sotsky, S. M., Krupnick, J. L., Martin, D. J., Sanislow, C. A., & Simmens, S. (2000). Relation of therapeutic alliance and perfectionism to outcome in brief outpatient treatment of depression. *Journal of Consulting and Clinical Psychology, 68*(1), 114–124. doi:10.1037/0022-006x.68.1.114

Zweben, J. E., Moses, Y., Cohen, J. B., Price, G., Chapman, W., & Lamb, J. (2015). Enhancing family protective factors in residential treatment for substance use disorders. *Child Welfare, 94*(5), 145–166. Retrieved from <Go to ISI>://WOS:000371000500010

6 Intervention Plans

6.1 Using Problems, Challenges, and Goals in Intervention Plans and Other Basics

To help clients overcome problems, meet challenges, and reach goals, social workers begin with a thoughtful intervention plan. An intervention plan is a contract or an agreement between a client and a social worker, typically requiring both of their signatures. In outpatient settings, it is important that client and social worker agree on the intervention plan. The plan must present the client's *goals* and *objectives*. Each goal should state broadly, in general terms, something the client wants to accomplish. Goals can provide the common thread weaving together the client's *challenges*. In this context, *challenge* has specialized meaning: a *challenge* is an action or a condition that, if achieved, helps the client overcome relevant problems (Miley, O'Melia, & DuBois, 2007). It is each action and condition on which the social worker must focus in order to foster future desirable behavior, *not* the client's current problem behavior. Take this example, for instance, of how social workers and clients think about problems, challenges, and goals as, together, they devise an intervention plan. A mother has a **problem** in that she habitually responds to her children's behavior with physical abuse. She also has a **problem** in that her family's home is unsanitary. This client's **challenges**, then, are to respond to or discipline her children using non-physical discipline and to maintain a sanitary residence. Given these problems and challenges, a **goal** laid out in this mother's intervention plan is to provide a safe environment for her children.

Usually, social workers readily identify problems and challenges of clients. Clients, families, can be overwhelmed by multiple problems, their abilities overshadowed by their weaknesses. Some clients' many weaknesses explain their problems rather obviously. But even for them, social workers must identify the **strengths** they *do* possess, strengths promising to help them overcome current problems and achieve each challenge noted in the intervention plan. Client strengths include holding a steady job, completing education, keeping children healthy, surviving trauma, having resolved earlier problems, and enjoying supportive relatives. Teaching clients about these strengths (and others) can foster hope, confidence, self-esteem, trust—any of which helps build client motivation and commitment concerning goals and challenges (Leung, Monit Cheung, & Stevenson, 1994).

Objectives are the building blocks of client goals. In setting the client's objectives, the social worker and client can make joint use of this basic formula: *Who will do what by when* (Miley, O'Melia, & DuBois, 2007). For instance, the intervention plan

DOI: 10.4324/9781003316688-6

objectives "Marie will yell at her brother no more than twice a week by June 22, 2023" and "Marie will play with her brother at least twice a week by June 22, 2023" identify *who* (the client, Marie), *what* (yell twice weekly or less at her brother; play with her brother twice a week or more), and *when* (by June 22, 2023). In an intervention plan, each objective must name a person whose behavioral change is desired; the client is very often the *who* named in the objective. The *will do what* in each objective calls for one single discrete, specific, observable, countable, and measurable behavior needing to be increased *or* decreased. A behavior in an objective can be measured by its frequency, as in our example of Marie yelling twice a week at most (time units other than "week" may serve here too, of course). Together, the client and social worker must determine a baseline frequency for each behavior measured by frequency. For instance, they might determine that Marie did not play with her brother at all and yelled at him on average seven times weekly.

When a behavior has great potential for harm, the objective should be to cease that behavior, not just decrease it; "Tom will stop using cocaine by February 10, 2023" is better than "Tom will reduce cocaine use to once a week by February 10, 2023." It is important as well to emphasize the word *do* in the formula for co-writing objectives with clients. To *do* a thing is to have that thing over and *done*—a state that lends itself naturally to being assessed—to check that thing off the list. A still-unfolding process is harder to assess. Thus "Tom will complete a drug treatment program by February 10, 2023" is a better objective than "Tom will attend a drug treatment program by February 10, 2023." In the latter, while technically the objective is achieved by mere attendance, presumably Tom wouldn't be helped much with problems or challenges if he attended, say, two times and then left treatment.

Finally, *by when* indicates the deadline client and social worker set for accomplishing an objective. A set date creates expectation and implies future review of behavior and change. Change *is* a process—but in this context a time-limited one. Sometimes, the *by when* date comes and goes with no achievement of the objective. When this happens, a new *by when* should be set by the client and social worker, indicating their agreement to some further period of intervention or treatment. Often, the *by when* is a function (at least in part) of treatment program policies or court mandates. With many support and self-help groups, including Alcoholics Anonymous (AA), a lengthy commitment is required, and "Tom will attend AA meetings regularly by February 10, 2023" is an appropriate objective (assuming Tom's social worker can confirm his regular attendance). But, just like the *will do what*, the *by when* must be uncompromising where behavior of clients might inflict harm. This makes "Carrie will cease physical discipline of her children immediately" the acceptable objective. Neither "Carrie will cease physical discipline of her children by August 5, 2023" (or *any* date in the future) nor "Carrie will reduce physical discipline of her children to once a week by August 5, 2023" works as an objective in an intervention plan. *Immediately* in the acceptable objective signifies the date the client and social worker sign their names to a mutually satisfactory intervention plan.

Any objective in an intervention plan should constitute a reasonable aim in light of the client's particular abilities and the availability and accessibility of services and resources. Moreover, working together the social worker and client should assign each of a plan's objectives the priority (or urgency) it merits. Objectives affecting safety are the most urgent; objectives affecting the degree of a client's pain or distress might come next.

Answering *Who will do what by when?* produces objectives, clearly. But objectives must then be accomplished, to avoid engaging in an empty exercise. Accomplishment of objectives is made doable by "translating" objectives into discrete tasks. In the example of Carrie, who aims to cease physical discipline of her children, that objective could realistically be advanced through such work as completing an anger management curriculum; learning about and using "I" messages; and mastering imagery techniques to deploy in response to anger-triggering events. Which task would Carrie take on first, most urgently? The answer requires weighing Carrie's preferences as well as the relative gravity of each challenge addressed by a task and the tasks' level of difficulty. For example, since Carrie is comfortable using imagery techniques to calm herself when angered, that task is taken on first. Next, she starts learning to use "I" messages to talk to her daughter. Last, Carrie completes that anger management curriculum.

It is important that social workers keep this in mind: Clients have expertise, too. Most indeed are experts on what they ultimately want, what they are willing to actually do, and what their capabilities actually are. A successful intervention plan relies heavily on all such expertise available from the client during collaboration with the social worker. Why? Because encouraging clients' self-determination nurtures growth of the strong working alliances that successful social workers desire. Putting clients to work developing the intervention plan shows respect, trust, and confidence in their capacity for change. Their initial participation inclines them toward continued participation. That can be backed up by regular reviews of clients' progress on their objectives, helping them stay motivated to succeed. Fairly typically, such a review takes place at each meeting or visit or session the client and social worker convene. Carrie's social worker, for instance, may ask her to describe some techniques she planned to learn and apply to manage her anger.

6.2 Individualized Service Plans versus Treatment Plans

Most often, social work in child welfare settings involves designing with clients intervention plans referred to as the *individualized service plan*, or *ISP*. In turn, in outpatient settings such as children and family services, social workers and their clients tend to be called on to design something called the *treatment plan*. Both the ISP and the treatment plan constitute the social worker's contract with the client, and both reflect generally the same type of goal-setting process, although ISPs do not outline tasks or activities leading to achievement of objectives. The two types of plan also differ in that ISPs are concerned with specifying objectives for individual family members' receipt of specific services, while treatment plans are concerned with specifying behavioral objectives for an individual. ISP and treatment plan worksheet along with instructions are provided in the next sections of this chapter.

6.3 ISP Worksheet, with Instructions

Objectives:

1 Explore solutions to public child-welfare dilemmas such as violence, addiction, homelessness, and mental illness.
2 Explore interventions available to families of at-risk children such as differential response, placement, foster care, family preservation, adoption, and permanency planning.

Instructions:

1 **Scenario:** Choose the case example the plan will be based on.
2 **Client Challenges and Strengths:** You and the client(s) list five challenges the client(s) in the case example is facing; as well, list five strengths the client(s) in the case example possesses.
3 **Individualized Service Plan (ISP):** Based on the challenges and strengths you and the client(s) identified, you and the client(s) determine a goal for the client(s) in the case example, along with three objectives linked to that goal, and then write an ISP that includes the client's prioritization of the three objectives. In writing the ISP, follow the format of the worksheet found on the following page.
4 **Building on Strengths:** For the client strengths you and client(s) listed, explain how a particular strength lends itself to the achievement of one objective you named for the client.

6.3.1 Individualized Service Plan

Strengths
1.
2.
3.
4.
5.
Challenges
1.
2.
3.
4.
5.
Goal: _____
_____

Objective #1: _____
Reasons: Explain this objective with the listed challenges and strengths of the client(s) <u>and</u> why it is the most important objective.
Objective #2: _____
Reasons: Explain this objective with the listed challenges and strengths of the client(s).
Objective #3: _____
Reasons: Explain this objective with the listed challenges and strengths of the client(s).

6.4 Treatment Plan Worksheet, with Instructions

Objectives:

1 Describe the evidence-supported models and methods of social work practice that serve children and adolescents and their families.
2 Social workers view themselves as learners, appreciate client cultural differences, and actively learn from their clients and colleagues.

Instructions and Requirements:

1   **Scenario:** Choose the case example the plan will be based on.
2   **Client Challenges and Strengths:** You and the client(s) list five challenges the client(s) in the case example is facing; as well, list five strengths the client(s) in the case example possesses.
3   **Treatment Plan:** Based on the challenges and strengths you and the client(s) identified, you and the client(s) determine a goal for the client(s) in the case example, along with 3–5 objectives linked to that goal, and then write a treatment plan that includes the client's prioritization of the 3–5 objectives. In writing the treatment plan, follow the format of the worksheet found on the following page.
4   **Tasks:** You and the client(s) identify three tasks the client(s) could use in achieving each of the three objectives.
5   **Building on Strengths:** For the client strengths you and client(s) listed, explain how a particular strength lends itself to the achievement of one objective you named for the client.

6.4.1 Treatment Plan

Strengths
1.
2.
3.
4.
5.
Challenges
1.
2.
3.
4.
5.
Goal: _____
_____
Objective #1: _____
Task #1: _____
Task #2: _____
Task #3: _____
Objective #2: _____
Task #1: _____
Task #2:_____
Task #3: _____
Objective #3: _____
Task #1: _____
Task#2: _____
Task #3: _____

References

Leung, P., Monit Cheung, K., & Stevenson, K. M. (1994). A strengths approach to ethnically sensitive practice for child protective service workers. *Child Welfare, 73,* 707.721

Miley, K. K., O'Melia, M., & DuBois, B. (2007). *Generalist Social Work Practice: An Empowering Approach.* Boston, MA: Allyn & Bacon.

7 Monitoring Progress

7.1 Self-Monitoring Techniques

Formulating an Individualized Service Plan (ISP) or Treatment Plan is a vital step in interventions. But no plan executes itself. And while the ISP or Treatment Plan indicates a client's intention, intention is no guarantee that objectives and goals will be attained (Gollwitzer & Sheeran, 2006; Harkin et al., 2016; Webb & Sheeran, 2006). If the objectives and goals of a plan specifies are to be met, the client must *act* according to the plan. Acting according to the plan—and meeting objectives—is promoted by frequent self-monitoring and collaborative monitoring of client's behavior and progress (Harkin et al., 2016). Frequent logging of target behaviors or expected behavior contributes to client awareness of any progress toward an objective (Balaghi et al., 2021). The use of self-monitoring logs and daily diaries has been shown to promote the desirable behavior of mothers and children involved in the child welfare system (Mathews, Fawcett, & Sheldon, 2009; Peterson, Tremblay, Ewigman, & Popkey, 2002) and other settings too (Balaghi et al., 2021; Feeney, 2021; Harkin et al., 2016; Minian, Lingam, deRuiter, Dragonetti, & Selby, 2021). Whenever feasible, clients should note target behavior in the log as soon as it occurs.

Social workers often provide clients with a self-monitoring log, facilitating clients' documentation of their own progress; Figure 7.1 is a good model. Target behavior can, obviously, be observed and recorded by clients themselves. It is sometimes helpful, however, for behavior to be observed and recorded by a parent, a partner, or another individual in the client's household or social network. The record of self-monitoring is established as the client recalls and writes down in the log pertinent instances of their own behavior. For instance, Marie is a client with an objective stating "Marie will yell at her brother no more than twice a week by June 22, 2023." Her self-monitoring log will thus contain numbers showing how many times each day Marie yelled at her brother, leading up to June 22, 2023. Marie is also working toward a second objective, namely, "Marie will play with her brother at least twice a week by June 22, 2023." Her log will thus contain Marie's documentation of the dates the two played together, leading up to June 22, 2023.

Research confirms that parents who participate in services they need have a relatively higher likelihood of reunifying with their children in the child welfare system (Cheng, 2010). Still, numbers of parents have shown resistance to such services when they perceive the services as something imposed on them from without, by social workers (Cheng & Lo, 2016). Using self-monitoring tends to counter such resistance to progress, because in documenting their desirable behavior, clients generate their

DOI: 10.4324/9781003316688-7

Target Behavior	Baseline						
	Day 1	Day 2	Day 3	Day 4	Day 5	Day 6	Day 7
	Intervention Phase						
	Day 1	Day 2	Day 3	Day 4	Day 5	Day 6	Day 7
	Day 8	Day 9	Day 10	Day 11	Day 12	Day 13	Day 14
	Day 15	Day 16	Day 17	Day 18	Day 19	Day 20	Day 21

Figure 7.1 Self-Monitoring Log.

own proof that they are learning and productively applying the necessary skills to solve problems. For example, Tom is a client pursuing an objective that says "Tom will complete a drug treatment program by February 10, 2023." For each day leading to February 10, Tom is charged with noting down in a self-monitoring log his application of the skills he is learning in treatment in order to achieve his objective; one sample skill is abstaining from drug use. Tom must also log the number of times he uses drugs. The documentation he creates in this way helps him to see any discrepancy between his objective and his daily behavior.

7.2 Baseline and Intervention Phase

Two phases of data collection should appear in the client's self-monitoring record. The first reflects *baseline* behavior. Information constituting the baseline documents a client's behavior prior to an intervention (Mathews et al., 2009; Smagner & Sullivan, 2005). Baseline measures can be recorded for a period of one to two weeks (Hartt & Waller, 2002). The second phase of data collection in the self-monitoring log reflects *intervention phase* behavior, in other words, instances of a target behavior once an intervention has started. In general, daily self-monitoring of intervention phase behavior requires three to eight weeks of data to illustrate client progress (Balaghi et al., 2021; Feeney, 2021; Rodriguez & Silvia, 2022; Smagner & Sullivan, 2005; Weltz, Armeli, Ford, & Tennen, 2016).

A client compiling baseline data will log the number of times each day the client demonstrated target behavior, across the seven to 14 days just preceding intervention. If the client and social worker want new practices to begin as close as possible to immediately, a week's worth of baseline data can be generated through client recall. Once the baseline record is complete, the client will record each day the number of times the target behavior was demonstrated that day; logging will persist for the initial three to eight weeks of the intervention phase. Tracking target behaviors as the intervention goes on brings the client evidence—of which, importantly, the client is the actor—that new skills and a desirable outcome are shaping up. Generating such evidence for themselves strengthens clients' self-confidence and reinforces their use of newly learned skills such as parenting skills.

Not uncommonly, documenting a target behavior in a self-monitoring logbook requires some clients to record more detailed information than simply a "count." A client with a baby experiencing failure-to-thrive might, for example, need to write down the time of each feeding as well as the number of ounces of formula the baby consumed at each feeding. Clients with depressive symptoms might, in turn, need to write down the time, duration, and circumstances of each crying spell they experience.

Again, whenever doing so is feasible, clients should record target behavior in the self-monitoring log immediately after the behavior has occurred. Some social workers and clients, furthermore, may opt to use a daily client diary to augment the log. Diary-keeping clients pause every evening to document personal feelings about the day's performance of newly learned skills and target behavior. Reflecting on emotions and other developments that informed the day's success (or apparent lack of success) may bring insights into things that foster and hinder the client's efforts to attain a desirable outcome (Harkin et al., 2016; Peterson et al., 2002).

7.3 Identifying Patterns of Behaviors and Behavioral Change

When the client has generated the self-documentation in the log and/or diary, reviewing all of it for signs of progress is essential. Such *progress reviews* will occur at intervals, the length of which depends on the urgency of the problem being addressed and on the specific social work services in place. The key requirement is that the client and social worker use every visit together to gauge the client's genuine progress and to review or reassess client goals and objectives. Progress reviews can be useful for determining whether an intervention merits continuation or whether modification of the intervention's ISP or Treatment Plan offers the better course. Such modification may involve adding new objectives to the plan or redefining its existing objectives.

A frequent result of a progress review is the identification of any pattern or patterns in data that has been recorded for the baseline and for intervention phase alike (Bloom, Fischer, & Orme, 2009). *Stable* behavior reflected by the data is one possible pattern; *increasing* and *decreasing* instances of a behavior are two more, while *fluctuation* in the measures of a behavior is another. How a pattern observed in client behavior is best interpreted hinges on the behavior's desirability or undesirability. An increasing number of recorded instances of desired behavior means progress toward objectives and goals. An increasing number of undesired behavior, however, means little progress or indeed worsening of the client's problem. Note that two significant assumptions underlie the self-monitoring process that is the focus of Chapter 7. The first assumption is that the social work intervention being implemented is the *cause* of any desired behavioral change logged beyond the baseline period. The second is that any desired change documented for the intervention phase will continue beyond that phase (Bloom et al., 2009).

Once the client and social worker have noted the patterns in the self-monitoring data, the progress review moves to comparison of the baseline behavior pattern with the intervention-phase behavior pattern. Comparison can help confirm that client problems are improving or worsening. Here is an example. The baseline for a client indicates a stable day-to-day pattern of *few* instances of a desired behavior. The intervention-phase daily log presents, in turn, a generally *increasing* number of instances of that behavior. Comparison of the two suggests behavioral improvement across the intervention phase to date. If the intervention-phase daily log were instead to present a generally *decreasing* number of instances of the behavior, comparison would suggest worsening of behavior across the intervention phase to date. Furthermore, even when self-monitoring gives an impression that progress is being made, additional, discrete behavioral challenges may crop up and call for plan modification in the form of new objectives supporting the client's goal.

As the client and social worker review the client's self-documented progress, the worker should offer encouragement and explore any newly available supports that might be brought to bear on the client's efforts to change behavior (Minian et al., 2021). For example, if reviewing intervention-phase data identifies either a worsening or fluctuating pattern, the social worker should invite the client to discuss any obstacles they suspect inhibit success in their demonstration of target behavior. After listening respectfully and considering potential solutions, the social worker might give constructive advice or take steps to secure additional resources helping the client overcome these obstacles. Progress reviews conducted in a genuinely collaborative spirit importantly bolster the client–worker working alliance.

References

Balaghi, D., Hierl, K., & Snyder, E. (2021). Self-monitoring for students with obsessive-compulsive disorder and autism spectrum disorder. *Intervention in School and Clinic*, 0(0), 10534512211047585. doi:10.1177/10534512211047585

Bloom, M., Fischer, J., & Orme, J. (2009). *Evaluating Practice: Guidelines for the Accountable Professional* (6th ed.). Needham Heights, MA: Allyn & Bacon.

Cheng, T. C. (2010). Factors associated with reunification: A longitudinal analysis of long-term foster care. *Children and Youth Services Review*, 32(10), 1311–1316. doi:10.1016/j.childyouth.2010.04.023

Cheng, T. C., & Lo, C. C. (2016). Linking worker-parent working alliance to parent progress in child welfare: A longitudinal analysis. *Children and Youth Services Review*, 71, 10–16. doi:10.1016/j.childyouth.2016.10.028

Feeney, D. M. (2021). Self-talk monitoring: A how-to guide for special educators. *Intervention in School and Clinic*, 0(0), 10534512211032575. doi:10.1177/10534512211032575

Gollwitzer, P. M., & Sheeran, P. (2006). Implementation intentions and goal achievement: A meta-analysis of effects and processes. *Advances in Experimental Social Psychology*, 38(6), 69–119, Academic Press. https://doi.org/10.1016/S0065-2601(06)38002-1

Harkin, B., Webb, T. L., Chang, B. P. I., Prestwich, A., Conner, M., Kellar, I., ... Sheeran, P. (2016). Does monitoring goal progress promote goal attainment? A meta-analysis of the experimental evidence. *Psychological Bulletin*, 142(2), 198–229. doi:10.1037/bul0000025

Hartt, J., & Waller, G. (2002). Child abuse, dissociation, and core beliefs in bulimic disorders. *Child Abuse & Neglect*, 26(9), 923–938. doi:10.1016/S0145-2134(02)00362-9

Mathews, T. L., Fawcett, S. B., & Sheldon, J. B. (2009). Effects of a peer engagement program on socially withdrawn children with a history of maltreatment. *Child & Family Behavior Therapy*, 31(4), 270–291. doi:10.1080/07317100903333160

Minian, N., Lingam, M., deRuiter, W. K., Dragonetti, R., & Selby, P. (2021). Co-designing behavior change resources with treatment-seeking smokers: Engagement events' findings. *Frontiers in Public Health*, 9. doi:10.3389/fpubh.2021.555449

Peterson, L., Tremblay, G., Ewigman, B., & Popkey, C. (2002). The parental daily diary: A sensitive measure of the process of change in a child maltreatment prevention program. *Behavior Modification*, 26(5), 627–647. doi:10.1177/014544502236654

Rodriguez, C. M., & Silvia, P. J. (2022). Spotlight on maternal perceptions of child behavior: A daily diary study with child welfare-involved mothers. *Behavioral Sciences*, 12(2), 44. Retrieved from https://www.mdpi.com/2076-328X/12/2/44

Smagner, J. P., & Sullivan, M. H. (2005). Investigating the effectiveness of behavioral parent training with involuntary clients in child welfare settings. *Research on Social Work Practice*, 15(6), 431–439. doi:10.1177/1049731505276994

Webb, T. L., & Sheeran, P. (2006). Does changing behavioral intentions engender behavior change? A meta-analysis of the experimental evidence. *Psychological Bulletin*, 132(2), 249–268. doi:10.1037/0033-2909.132.2.249

Weltz, S. M., Armeli, S., Ford, J. D., & Tennen, H. (2016). A daily process examination of the relationship between childhood trauma and stress-reactivity. *Child Abuse & Neglect*, 60, 1–9. doi:10.1016/j.chiabu.2016.08.005

About the Author

My work with over 300 families from diverse ethnic backgrounds has brought me wide-ranging experiences addressing child abuse and neglect, juvenile delinquency, mental health, and suicide issues affecting families in the United States. I was in clinical practice as a licensed social worker for eight years after completing my doctoral study in social work. Working for agencies in Ohio and Michigan, I provided intensive family-preservation programs in cases involving child abuse and neglect, and I provided counseling for alternative-school students. I was for a time a Chicago-based child welfare worker with the Illinois Department of Children and Family Services. I also served as a community organizer in Chicago's Chinatown, charged with facilitating immigrant families' participation in reforming local schools.

I am, furthermore, fully familiar with the expectations and requirements for educating competent professional social workers, having a long background in leadership in social work education. I directed the BSW program at the University of Alabama at Birmingham and the MSW program at the University of Alabama. I chaired the Department of Social Work and Human Services at Kennesaw State University in Georgia and the Department of Social Work and Child Advocacy at Montclair State University in New Jersey. In Alabama, I worked to strengthen university social work programs' collaborative role with professionals from the state's child protective services agency, via a Title IV-E project. I also served on the quality-assurance committees of two Alabama counties' child protective services agencies.

My teaching experiences over two decades were numerous. I conducted undergraduate and graduate courses in social work practice, human behavior and the social environment, research methods, and social welfare policy. My courses were well received by students, who seemed to appreciate my use of case scenarios like those in this book, drawn from my work as a field social worker.

My curriculum vitae lists 111 published and forthcoming works (I am the sole or first author of 65). All but eight of the listed works were published in journals having impact factors; I have acquired an h-index score of 18, and my publications to date represent 767 citations. In 2011, the University of Alabama School of Social Work honored me with its Dean's Faculty Award for Research, Teaching, and Service.

Index

For Product Safety Concerns and Information please contact our EU
representative GPSR@taylorandfrancis.com
Taylor & Francis Verlag GmbH, Kaufingerstraße 24, 80331 München, Germany

www.ingramcontent.com/pod-product-compliance
Lightning Source LLC
Chambersburg PA
CBHW080134270326
41926CB00021B/4486

9 781032 327549